PRAISE FOR YASMIN'S FIRST BOOK,

THE BLUEPRINT FOR MY GIRLS

"Yasmin Shiraz answers the questions the way that we all wish we could have had them answered for us when we were growing up. *Blueprint* is strong and direct and yet sprinkled with all of the nurturing and love that can inspire these young women to discover and develop their beauty—inside and out."

—BET.com

"I highly recommend *The Blueprint for My Girls*, as it taught me to have a very positive self-image and it allows me to be who I am. I respect Yasmin Shiraz for being so brave in writing this book and sharing her emotions."

—Kyla Pratt, actress

"This book is a beautiful tool for the continuation of the restoration of pride into our young women."

—India.Arie, singer/songwriter

"Yasmin Shiraz has written an excellent book filled with everyday wisdom and commonsense advice. Although this book would be great for any woman to read, it is a must for teenagers and young adults. After you're finished reading *The Blueprint for My Girls*, you will be amazed how much wisdom is packed into such a short book."

—*Right On!* magazine

"[*The Blueprint for My Girls*] informs, motivates, inspires, and comforts."

—*Blackgirl Magazine*

"*The Blueprint for My Girls* is an inspirational book that does exactly what it promises: shows the reader how to become the woman she aspires to be. Shiraz challenges the reader to ask herself hard questions and change her life accordingly. What I loved most is that it demands that the reader take responsibility for her life but it is communicated in a kind and embracing manner."

—Rosalind Wiseman, author of *Queen Bees & Wannabes*

"Shiraz's book of 99 affirmations does get essential points across. *Blueprint* provides many springboards for self-exploration."

—Rebecca Louie, *Daily News*

"Yasmin Shiraz coaches girls and sets them off on the road leading to strong women who navigate life on their own terms. Offering first-hand experience and proactive advice on how to ride out life's bumps and surprises, she points the way to an empowered life full of courage, determination, and self-love."

—Erzsi Deàk, editor of *Period Pieces*

"Yasmin has put together this easy-to-read book that girls can keep handy as they make critical choices and shape their futures."

—Catherine Dee, author of *The Girls' Book of Success* and *The Girls' Book of Wisdom*

"While this book is targeted at young females, some of the lessons might also ring true for the mature woman. *The Blueprint for My Girls* is one of those books that can enlighten those of us who believe that we have learned all there is to learn about life."

—DallasBlack.com

"I recommend this book to girls of all ages. It's a useful road map for things women usually have to learn the hard way . . . by making mistakes."

—Olivia, singer/songwriter

the BLUEPRINT for my Girls in Love

99 Rules for Dating, Relationships, and Intimacy

YASMIN SHIRAZ

A FIRESIDE BOOK
Published by Simon & Schuster
New York   London   Toronto   Sydney

Names and identifying characteristics of people in this book
have been changed.

FIRESIDE
Rockefeller Center
1230 Avenue of the Americas
New York, NY 10020

For information regarding special discounts for bulk purchases,
please contact Simon & Schuster Special Sales at 1-800-456-6798
or business@simonandschuster.com

Designed by Jaime Putorti

Manufactured in the United States of America

10   9   8   7   6   5   4   3   2

Library of Congress Cataloging-in-Publication Data
Shiraz, Yasmin.
     The blueprint for my girls in love: 99 rules for dating, relationships,
and intimacy / Yasmin Shiraz.
          p.   cm.
"A Fireside book."
Includes index.
     1. Dating (Social cutoms) 2. Interpersonal relations in adolescence.
3. Sexual ethics for teenagers. 4. Teenage girls—Psychology. I. Title.
HQ801.S5278   2005   306.73'083'2—dc22   2005042617

ISBN 0-7432-7096-7

For Mary Anne, Macoia, and all of "My Girls" worldwide: No two people see love through the same eyes, nor do two people feel love through the same heart.

Acknowledgments

You never know how your experiences will help you later in life or assist others in their journey. Having the idea to write the Blueprint for My Girls series has been a twofold blessing. It has allowed me to heal from old wounds and has permitted others to learn from my mistakes as well as my triumphs.

I have to thank my friends, family, and acquaintances whose stories inspire these pages as much as mine. Our friendships over the years have been interesting, fun, and definitely a learning experience. All of the advice that I've given and all of the advice that I received I earnestly tried to put in this book. Who would have thought testimony from our first dates could be of use to anyone? Remember, they're laughing with us!

I thank my husband for giving me space to write and be who I am. He's never asked me to be anybody else, which in turn encourages me to continue to grow as a person. Plus, he's part of the best relationship that I've ever had.

Sometimes when I don't have the energy to write, my daughter rallies me and says stuff like, "Mom, you can do it. This will be a good book." My daughter is always there, cheering me on in whatever task that lies ahead. Thanks,

Macoia! Years from now when Macoia is a teenager herself I hope she can appreciate *The Blueprint for My Girls in Love.*

I want to thank my son, Yamir, for always reminding me to laugh, smile and be lighthearted. I plan to distribute this book to any and all potential girlfriends of my son, complete with quiz. He's not quite two years old yet, but I must be prepared.

I want to thank my dad for reading and rereading and reading again *The Blueprint for My Girls* and believing in my talents as an author. He's even talked to his coworkers about my books. It's incredible to receive that kind of admiration from a parent. Additionally, my father has always been kind and loving toward me, no matter the mistakes that I've made in my life.

I want to thank my mom and her husband for supporting my work through their book club, babysitting duties, and being generally great people. There's no *I* in team, and they're a great part of my team.

To "My Girls" all over the world, I thank you and love all of your e-mails and letters. Thank you for coming to my book signings and talking to me. I cherished our conversations. All of the organizations and churches that have been instrumental in assisting girls in various ways, bless you and thank you for supporting the Blueprint for My Girls series.

All of the media outlets that have featured me as a guest or featured my first book, *The Blueprint for My Girls: How to Build a Life Full of Courage, Determination, & Self-Love,* thank you. I know you have proposals coming to you from every direction. Thanks for welcoming me to your audience.

I thank my Simon & Schuster family for their editorial and public relations support. Your assistance in opening the doors for the Blueprint for My Girls series has been incredible.

There have been times when I didn't know where the road would take me, but I had faith. There have been times when I felt I should be like others in order to be happy, successful, or beautiful, then I realized that God made me unique. I thank God for my triumphs and my tragedies, my good days and my bad—they all contribute to the source from which I write. Thank you, God; thank you, all.

Contents

Introduction

J always refer to my first book, *The Blueprint for My Girls: How to Build a Life Full of Courage, Determination, and Self-Love,* as the gift that keeps on giving. When I wrote it, I had to dig deep into my past, and it was therapy for my soul: my first gift. When it was published and "my girls" wrote letters saying how the book helped them, that was my second gift. But then, unexpectedly, girls, mothers, parents, teachers, and others started showing up at my book signings and requesting that I host workshops at their churches, schools, and social organizations. Those gifts keep on coming.

While I was on tour for my first book, young women often brought up relationships, dating, and intimate situations. These conversations made me realize what I needed to write next: a book that addresses the tough questions that teen girls are asking about dating, relationships, and intimacy. Each situation in this book is presented as a question, answered with a rule and testimony, then reaffirmed with a blueprint.

As young women, we date, we love, and we experience life with our hearts set to be fulfilled. Yet too often, our exposed hearts are left empty. In my journey from teenager to young college student, no single experience impacted my self-esteem like being in an abusive relationship, being pressured in sexual situations, or being uneducated concerning such matters. I know from conducting workshops with teens that many of you are struggling with relationships and sex, partly because you aren't receiving good information on your options. In every city I've visited, there is a disturbing underlying theme: girls should accept whatever dating situation or relationship that comes their way, even if it is less than what they want, even if it's less than what they deserve. This is why this book is necessary.

I cherish my role as your big sister—old enough to advise you, young enough to keep it real. When I've bonded with many of you on the road, it has lifted my spirit. As we met in various cities, schools, and after-school programs, I've noticed how we bend like the grass. We're flexible even when it hurts us. We are always bending to make someone else feel comfortable, often forgetting that we have a responsibility to make ourselves comfortable. In our roles of supporting and loving others, we are becoming disconnected with self and becoming unfamiliar with a strong sense of who we are. *The Blueprint for My Girls in Love* is your guidebook to staying grounded and fortified as you experience dating, relationships, and intimacy.

The subtitle of this book is *99 Rules for Dating, Relationships, and Intimacy.* These are rules that shouldn't be broken if you want to retain self-respect, maintain high self-esteem, and experience life with as much enjoyment as possible. The 99 Testimonies that are shared in this book are separated into three chapters, "Dating," "Relationships," and "Intimacy." It is my belief that you should date before you have a relationship, and that you should have a committed relationship with someone before the two of you become intimate. When I was preparing to write *The Blueprint for My Girls in Love*, I reread some of my old diaries, questioned some high school and college friends, and put my memory to work. As a result, I've written 99 situations inspired by what my friends, my relatives, and I have experienced. It is my desire that you learn from these experiences so that you'll be able to make the best choices for you.

So many of you have told me that when you ask somebody about sex, that person assumes that you are already involved in those kinds of things. The result is a lot of you aren't asking questions even though you desperately need answers. At the end of the book, I've included a list of the people who you should be able to talk to without feeling "guilty" of anything. I've also included a list of organizations that I've worked with and/or am familiar with who help young people. We want more communication, feedback, and answers.

I have also included a list of different kinds of birth control and how they work in the back of the book. Many girls don't know about various birth control methods even though they've decided to engage in sexual behavior. I want you to know what you're getting yourself into. I'm not advocating that you become sexually active, but I believe you should be educated about birth control methods.

Many issues in this book are inspired by situations that my friends, family, and I wish never happened. But they did happen. Some bad experiences occurred because we didn't stand up for ourselves. Some of our hearts were broken because we wanted to be associated with a person who really didn't care about us. We were scarred emotionally because we didn't stop to take a moment to think about our own self-preservation or what made us happy. Some of our trauma occurred because we rushed into situations that we were not emotionally prepared for. Instead of thinking or acting in ways to propel ourselves forward or to simply feel good about who we were, we spent more time accepting bad treatment from somebody else. That is no way to live.

This book of ninety-nine rules is about you having more, not accepting less. Girls are worthy of having more respect, more love, more positive experiences. This book is about my girls being strong, being decisive, and navigating their lives in an empowered, enlightened, and joy-filled way. We are not victims. We will not allow anyone to make us victims. As you read *The Blueprint for My Girls in Love*, be encouraged that you have your entire life ahead of you, and though you will make mistakes, know that I believe in your strength and in your future. No one defines your life but you.

Your girl,
Yasmin Shiraz

PHASE 1

Dating

The beginning phase of every good relationship is the time in which you get to know each other. In this phase you learn about each other's thoughts, fears, and feelings. It's the foundation of a relationship that could blossom in the future. Without any pressures or expectations, dating can be a rewarding experience.

How will I ever get a boyfriend if
all the girls in school are prettier or
dress better than I do?

_____

rule 1

Comparing yourself to other girls is a dead end.

She sits across from you in math class. Every time you have on a new outfit, so does she. Every time you come to school with a fly hairdo, she arrives the next day with an even better one. It seems like everything you do, she's doing, and everything you want to do, she's doing. You can't outdo her, but it seems like she's outdoing you without any effort. But there's one point that you're forgetting: your life is not about the girl in math class. Your life is not about anybody but you. The only person that you should ever be willing to compare yourself to is YOU. And not only that, the person that you are comparing yourself to is probably also comparing herself to you. No matter how perfect someone seems on the outside, everyone has insecurities. The key is to get over them and love yourself anyway.

MY TESTIMONY

I'm five-three, and I used to be obsessed with being taller. It seemed to me that girls who were three or four inches taller looked so much better in their clothes. In high school, I worried about the length of my hair. It was shoulder length, but if I looked at a girl whose hair was longer, I felt that my hair was not long enough. When I started dating, I compared myself to other girls even more because I wanted to know what kind of girls guys liked. But when I reached my junior year in high school, I decided to focus on the things that I felt made me stand out and feel good about me. I began to cherish certain aspects about myself that I hadn't seemed to care about before, like my smile, having dimples, the natural waves in my hair. Then I started getting compliments on my hairstyles, the clothes that I wore, and how I carried myself. The more I took interest in myself, the more I realized that God created me the way He wanted me to be. And if guys weren't gonna like me for who I was, then they didn't deserve me anyway.

BLUEPRINT

I can't focus on what other girls look like. God made me the way that I am.

YOUR TESTIMONY

Is there a girl who you often compare yourself to at school? Put yourself in her shoes and make a list of the things she probably admires about you.

What should I say if someone asks me if I'm a virgin?

rule 2

Your virginity is nobody's business but yours.

*I*n the information-driven era that we live in, people want to know every detail about you. But whether you've had sex or not is a very personal matter, and no one else's concern. Fifty girls might yell their sexual status up and down the hall, but that doesn't mean you have to. It's personal, and not everyone can be trusted to keep your confidence. If someone asks you and you don't want to reveal it to them, say, "That's a personal question, and no offense, but it's none of your business."

MY TESTIMONY

Several friends of mine and I would occasionally sit in our dorm room and talk about boys, school, dating, and so on. My friend Jade never really talked about her personal life with us. She gave an opinion on our lives but didn't share much of hers. We figured she was an ultra-private person and left it at that. During our freshman year, a guy from the track team started liking her. Within a week, Jade wrote him a letter telling him all of her personal business, including detailed information regarding her virginity. Minutes after reading the letter, he was on the phone telling people that he couldn't believe that Jade hadn't experienced sex yet. Worst yet, he was going down his dorm hallway reading her letter to anyone who would listen. Her sexual experience wasn't our business, or his either—to say nothing of the others he'd told.

BLUEPRINT

My sexual status is my private business. I'm not ashamed of it, but I don't have to feel pressured to discuss it.

YOUR TESTIMONY

Make your own "I will not discuss" list. These are personal details that you would feel embarrassed by if a complete stranger knew.

I will not discuss . . .

How do I make
a good first impression?

---

rule 3

Take your personal hygiene seriously.

When you're dating, you're speaking to people up close—breathing in people's faces, in fact. Your hormones are working overtime, and so are your sweat glands. Breath mints and deodorant should be a staple for any teen who wants to date. Your dating years aren't the time to skimp on the fluoride or be chintzy with the soap. There's nothing worse than poor personal hygiene for killing a potential date.

MY TESTIMONY

When I was in high school, me and some of my friends participated in pep block. Pep block was the school's cheering section that didn't include cheerleaders. I recall being at a pep block meeting that was held during the same time that the basketball team practiced. One of the guys from the team came up to my friend Lizette. Rumors had been circulating for the past week or so that he liked her, and he felt that seeing Lizette after practice would be the perfect introduction. Not. When he walked over to Lizette, he was dripping sweat from his forehead and, judging from her facial expressions, he smelled pretty bad. She didn't want to brush him off, but trying to talk with someone for the first time when you are sweating and funky is not a good thing.

BLUEPRINT

In making first impressions, personal hygiene should always be in check.

YOUR TESTIMONY

I can improve my personal hygiene by . . .

There's a guy in my neighborhood who has asked me out a couple of times. He's eighteen, and I'm fourteen. Do you think he's too old for me?

---

rule 4

Some guys are too old for you.

a guy that's four or more years older than you has probably experienced a whole lot more than you. It's likely that he'll expect things from you that you aren't ready for. A girl who's fourteen and just left eighth grade is thinking about relationships in a far different manner than the guy who is eighteen and already is legally an adult. A twelve-year-old shouldn't be rushed into experiencing situations that are comfortable for a sixteen-year-old. Age differences in the teen years speak more to various level of experiences than any particular number. A seventeen-year-old who has gone to the prom has a different experience set than a thirteen-year-old who is just entering high school. Experience makes all the difference.

MY TESTIMONY

When I was fifteen, I went out with a nineteen-year-old, and it was one of the worst experiences of my teenage years. I felt pressured to have sex and drink alcohol. While I was worrying about what my parents would say about certain things, he thought about what police officers would do if they found out he broke the law. Our thought processes and concerns were completely different. He didn't respect himself, and he often made demeaning comments to me. He lied about everything, from where he was going to who he was with or what he wanted from me. Being inexperienced, I never knew that a guy could be so deceitful and full of himself. If I had had this relationship just two years later, I wouldn't have taken such a hit to my self-esteem as I did at fifteen.

BLUEPRINT

I will not be in a relationship with someone who can take advantage of my lack of experience.

YOUR TESTIMONY

If you want to figure out if a guy is too old for you, make a list of the things you both have in common. Then think about what your top priorities will be in six months. Are the lists still the same?

What is true love?

---

rule 5

True love is more than an emotion. It's action and commitment.

*W*e often hear about people being in love or loving someone. In those cases, love is best described as an emotion or a state of feeling. But love is more than how you feel. It is also how you act toward your loved ones. Love will move you to do things in a way that "like" will not. The ultimate reward of love is commitment. More than a relationship, commitment involves people being dedicated, involved, and loyal to each other.

MY TESTIMONY

I first experienced true love my junior year in college. I had met this nice guy during my second semester as a sophomore. He was polite, kind, and easy to talk to. Over the summer we kept in touch and built our friendship, and I literally counted down the days until we'd both be back on campus. When we arrived at Hampton University and we saw each other for the first time in three months, we hugged each other like long-lost buddies. Our connection was emotional, and I felt a sense of warmth around him. When we decided to make our relationship official, we were committed to spending time and supporting each other's needs. There were times when our schedules conflicted and the demands of schoolwork interrupted our "quiet time," but even then we shared a desire to be with each other and acted in each other's best interests most of the time.

BLUEPRINT

I understand that true love is more than butterflies in my stomach and a warm feeling in my chest.

YOUR TESTIMONY

What types of things could your boyfriend do that would show you that he truly loved you?

All the girls in my school want to date the most popular guy in our class.

Why is that?

___

rule 6

Dating a popular person at school doesn't guarantee happiness or even acceptance to the "it" crowd.

*H*e's the star of the basketball team. He's the president of the student council. Everybody in school wants to be his friend. A popular boy attracts more girls than a lip gloss giveaway. But what does popularity really say about the man? Does it mean that he's nice to girls? Does it mean that he would be a great boyfriend? Does it mean that he doesn't use drugs? Does it mean that he's a law-abiding, upstanding citizen? Absolutely not. Popularity means nothing except that the person is known by others. Many girls are attracted to the most popular boys because they believe it says something about who they are. And for that moment, it does say something. It says: "You're Mr. Popular's girlfriend." But remember, that title only lasts as long as the relationship.

MY TESTIMONY

When I was in high school, the most popular jacket to have was the high school state champion basketball jacket. If you wore this jacket, you were the envy of other girls because the basketball players were the most popular guys in the whole state. My boyfriend Londell had one of these jackets. I didn't ask him to wear his jacket, he asked me to wear it. I didn't see it as a big deal. The first time I wore Londell's jacket, I could hear girls whisper, "Whose jacket does she have on?" as I walked by. When I attended basketball games with this jacket on, everybody in the gym knew that I was the star's girlfriend. I must admit, though, not everybody liked me because of that jacket, and some people absolutely didn't like me because of it. And when we broke up I gave him back his jacket, and the people who liked me because of who I was dating shifted their interest from me to his new girlfriend.

BLUEPRINT

I will choose who I date by how much I like the guy, not by how much others like him.

YOUR TESTIMONY

What personality traits would you like in a boyfriend?

True or false?
Girls are a lot more sensitive
than boys are.

_____

rule **7**

Though most guys would never admit it, their feelings are hurt fairly easily.

Call it male ego or testosterone-charged bravado, a boy who is turned down by a girl isn't going to show that his feelings are hurt. Maybe he'll start telling the world that he didn't really like her, or maybe he'll spread rumors about her. The fact is, most guys can't conceive that a particular girl that they are interested in doesn't want to be bothered with them. A simple "I'd rather just be friends" can become a year-long nightmare because of a bruised ego. So when you have to rebut a male suitor, remember to be gentle.

MY TESTIMONY

Tim was crazy about Clarisse. He wrote her letters, gave her stuffed animals, and treated her to whatever movie was out at the time. Clarisse was flattered by Tim's interest, but we often talked about how she didn't want to be in a relationship with him. Although Clarisse explained this to Tim many times, he was undeterred by her chilly demeanor toward him. He continued to express his feelings to Clarisse and felt confident that he'd eventually win her over. All the girls couldn't believe how much Tim wanted to be in a relationship with Clarisse. One day on the phone, after Clarisse had a bad day, she told him flat-out, "I don't like you because you act too goofy. You wear clothes that someone's grandfather would wear." When Clarisse told me that she'd said that, I said, "You didn't really say that. Stop playin'." But she had said it. After that conversation, Tim never called Clarisse again. I suppose their last discussion bruised his ego too severely.

BLUEPRINT

I will attempt to be sensitive to the male ego in situations that call for it.

YOUR TESTIMONY

Make a list of ways you can turn down a date with someone that aren't lies but won't be too harsh.

There's a guy I really like,
but he doesn't know that I'm alive.
How do I get him to notice me?

---

rule 8

Getting somebody's attention requires tact and honesty.

e want to get to know a person who we've seen at a school event, at the mall, or at lunch. At the same time, we don't want to seem foolish in approaching someone that we don't know. The best approach is to be honest, up-front. You might consider calmly introducing yourself and taking your time to strike up a conversation about something you both have in common.

MY TESTIMONY

Is there a course harder than college-level geometry to a person who doesn't love math? I don't think so. When I was enrolled in geometry, I made a point of sitting at the front of the class, listening intently to the professor so I wouldn't miss a thing. One day after class a guy named Darryl walked up to me on campus and asked me how I liked geometry. I had never seen him before, but I told him that I was struggling in the course. When I asked him how did he know that I had geometry, he told me that we were in the same class together. I guess I hadn't noticed him because I was so focused on trying to pass the course. After the semester was over, Darryl told me that he wanted to meet me from the first time he saw me in geometry class. Because of the way that he approached me, we developed a great friendship, and I've always had respect for him.

BLUEPRINT

I don't have to be afraid to introduce myself to new people as long as I am real in my approach.

YOUR TESTIMONY

What's the worst that could happen if I walk up to someone and say . . .

Why does it seem like some girls get all the guys?

---

rule 9

Some girls do get all the guys.

*I*t seems that some girls never have a problem finding a boyfriend. Even before one breakup happens, she's wearing another guy's jacket at school. Call it luck or call it a curse, you never know what's going on behind the scenes. You can't worry about other girls and their boyfriends. And anyway, who's to say if the girl who gets all the guys is even happy?

MY TESTIMONY

When I was in high school, a girl named ShaiLynn used to get all the guys. It seemed that all the boys—popular, athletic, and otherwise—were waiting in line for the chance to date her. She was petite, with a cute face and wavy hair. Boys from my school and other schools fought over her. She had a certain look about her, and the boys in my school obsessed over her. ShaiLynn was close to one of my friends and was always complaining about her various boyfriends. From the outside other girls envied the attention that Shai-Lynn got from all of those boys. But they didn't know how ShaiLynn was always down on herself when a guy didn't do exactly what she wanted. They didn't understand that when ShaiLynn wasn't with a guy, she couldn't stand to be by herself.

BLUEPRINT

I'm not gonna worry about who is dating who. I have enough on my plate just thinking about my life.

YOUR TESTIMONY

How would your life change if you suddenly had a new boyfriend every two weeks?

There are a bunch of guys at school who are loud and bully girls in the hallway. One of the boys in the group likes me. Should I give him a chance?

_____

rule 10

Disrespectful boys are losers.

*H*e tries to cop a feel when you walk by his locker. He calls a girl who doesn't want to give him her phone number a whore. He walks around the school like he's mad at the world. He rolls with a bunch of guys who are just like him—quick to diss, easy to anger, and hard to appreciate. Guys like this are not going anywhere, and they probably know it. Maybe that's why they're so pissed off.

MY TESTIMONY

In my eighth-grade summer program, there was a guy who was so cute the girls in the program didn't even refer to him by name. Most of us giggled behind his back and called him "the cute boy." One day on the back of a hot bus, he was touching and feeling on Kelly, a girl from camp. He was groping her breasts and buttocks, and if he saw anyone looking at him, he just smiled. The girl, Kelly, was so glad that Leon was taking time with her that she didn't care that his actions made her look like a skank. A week later Leon and Kelly were on bad terms, and he sat behind her on that same bus and called her a whore until the bus dropped her home. As me and some of my other friends heard her crying, we rolled our eyes at Leon and never looked at him the same again. From that moment, he was the ugliest boy in the summer program.

BLUEPRINT

I will not associate with disrespectful guys. They have nothing to offer me.

YOUR TESTIMONY

I think it's disrespectful when guys . . .

How do I know for sure that a guy's not interested in dating me?

---

rule 11

If he keeps brushing you off, he's probably not interested.

*Y*ou've given him your phone number, and maybe he's given you his. But when you call him, he doesn't have anything to say. He rushes you off the phone and doesn't call you back. You keep calling and standing by his locker. You continue to show up at places that you know you'll see him. He gives you the cold shoulder. His actions are saying that he's not interested in you, so you should take a hint and move on. Some people will never come out and say, "I don't like you like that," but they'll give us clues as if we were Sherlock Holmes. Take a hint.

MY TESTIMONY

I guess it was how Sherman looked at me in our high school English class. Maybe it was his corny jokes that he always told only me, or the fact that he was concerned about my mood swings. I knew that he liked me because a regular guy doesn't show that much interest. But I wasn't attracted to him in a "boyfriend" way. He was nice, friendly, and smart, but he just wasn't my type. When Sherman suggested datelike things to me, I ignored them, but I was still friendly with him. Just because I didn't want him to be my boyfriend didn't mean I wanted him to hate me. After a while Sherman caught the hint, and we remained friends throughout high school.

BLUEPRINT

I will not continue to waste time being interested in someone who isn't interested in me. Some things are not meant to be.

YOUR TESTIMONY

I think I was given a hint when . . .

Adults are always telling me to "love myself," but what does that really mean? I don't want to be conceited. And what does self-love have to with dating anyway?

rule 12

Self-love impacts every relationship that you will ever have.

*L*oving yourself is taking care of you, making sure that you're not hurting, keeping yourself protected and happy. It's like walking around being pro-you. When you take time to treat yourself well, you will know how to respect and treat others. Self-love is different from being conceited in that conceit focuses on an exaggerated opinion of who you think you are, and self-love focuses on action, specifically how you treat yourself. Your relationships with friends and loved ones will reflect how you love yourself, because you are only willing to give to others what you have already given yourself.

MY TESTIMONY

In my junior and senior years of college, I was recovering from a series of disappointing relationships. When I first began dating the man who I would later marry, I was just finishing college. Still bruised from previous situations, I didn't always treat him with the care and respect he deserved. As our union progressed and I was healed from old wounds, I realized that while I was hurting, it was difficult for me to give love to someone else. During my lowest emotional moments, I did not have the heart to care for my friends or family like I should have. But the more I became in touch with myself and cared about what happened to me, the better I treated everyone in my circle.

BLUEPRINT

Loving myself will help me know how to treat others. I will strive to love myself more.

YOUR TESTIMONY

List the five things you can do this week to promote your well-being.

Are all smart girls lonely? I don't want to spend so much time on my schoolwork that I graduate from high school without ever going on a date.

---

rule 13

Focusing on schoolwork instead of boys is not a crime.

*P*eople often look at the girl with her nose in the books and think she doesn't have a boyfriend because no one wants a studyholic girlfriend. Not true. Smart girls who focus on their work are asked out on dates all the time. Some even socialize. But there are girls who prefer books to boys. They'd rather concentrate on finishing high school and getting into college than worrying about wearing somebody's class ring. Look at it this way, the girl with her nose in the books is allowing her schoolwork to be the down-payment on the Mercedes-Benz she'll be driving ten years from now.

MY TESTIMONY

Angie played basketball and stayed on the honor roll. When there were parties or get-togethers, Angie never attended. She was either preparing for a basketball game or preparing for class. Unlike many of her teammates, she took her practice philosophy and applied it to her life. She trained for basketball games every day by running, lifting weights, and exercising. She trained for tests every day by studying and going to the library even when there was no pending examination. Ten years after graduation, Angie was no longer playing basketball, but she was running operations at a Fortune 500 company. In a short time, she was earning a salary that few people will ever attain. I've reconnected with Angie since high school, and though she is now married, she is glad that she made her schoolwork her priority. Her priorities paved the way for a stable future.

BLUEPRINT

When I choose to pick schoolwork over socializing, I'm selecting a path of success for my life.

YOUR TESTIMONY

I want to be successful in . . .

The guys at school are so corny.
Why are they so immature?

_____

rule 14

Boys mature more slowly than girls.

*J*t's a universal accepted fact: boys don't mature at the same rate as girls. What does this mean for a sixteen-year-old girl who is dating a sixteen-year-old boy? Well, since maturity affects emotions and sense of self, a sixteen-year-old boy will often deny his feelings or be completely controlled by them. A sixteen-year-old boy will not have the grasp of dating or relationships that a girl will who is the exact same age. Is this fair? I doubt it, but it's life.

MY TESTIMONY

Tony was a guy I went to college with who wanted us to date. Because I didn't find him attractive or remotely inter-esting, I didn't want to date him. If I saw him on campus, I engaged in polite conversation, but I didn't pretend to want to hang out with him. If Tony called my dorm, I kept our discussions short. On a couple of occasions he asked about my personal life and if I had a boyfriend. I told him I didn't have a boyfriend, and I wasn't trying to enlist him. Well, one day after class, I was talking to one of my platonic guy friends and Tony rode by. He gave me an accusatory look and sped off. That evening he had someone drop off a box of fake doo-doo to my dorm room. It had a note that read, "Because you're such a shit . . ." Now, how immature is that? After I got over the initial shock of his immature behavior, I was pleasantly relieved that I had not gone out with him. I thought to myself over and over again, if I was the subject of cruel accusations and offensive gifts and we were just friends, what would I have been in for if we had actually gone out on a date?

BLUEPRINT

I realize that guys are different from girls and may not understand situations on the same maturity level that I do.

YOUR TESTIMONY

I noticed the difference between guys and girls when . . .

What is lust?

---

rule 15

Lust is desire that fades like red dye on a cheap T-shirt.

*Y*ou may have had an article of clothing that you wanted very badly. You many have been willing to work extra hard at odd jobs in order to get it. Some people lust for clothes, purses, or boys. Lust is a strong emotion. But unlike love, there's no real commitment when it comes to lust. Whatever happened to your favorite jeans from the eighth grade? By the time you enter the eleventh grade, you probably won't even remember what they look like. They will be out of style. Lust is similar. You like something a lot for a short amount of time, and then the feeling just fades—boys included.

MY TESTIMONY

House music was the tune d'jour when I was in college. The vibes from the music seemed to energize the crowd like a gigantic battery. But not everybody could dance to house music, me included. Above-average coordination and bodily rhythm was necessary to dance to that kind of music. At a Virginia Union party, I saw a guy on the dance floor who was working his house steps like Usher works music videos. His moves were effortless and sensual at the same time. I had to get to know this guy. Through a mutual friend, I met Dylan. And for about three weeks, I thought he was really hot. Whenever I heard house music, I was glad to know him. Funny, though—whenever the music was off, he became an annoying, unattractive character without a sound track.

BLUEPRINT

Lust can trip me up if I'm not careful. Before I become crazed about anything, I'll let some time pass.

YOUR TESTIMONY

Think back to four years ago. Was there an object or a person that you couldn't live without? What role does that object or person play in your life now?

My mom doesn't allow me to accept expensive gifts from guys. What's the big deal? If they want to spend their money like that, why should I stop them?

---

rule 16

Expensive gifts usually carry an unspoken meaning or expectation.

If one guy gives you a leather jacket for your birthday, and another guy gives you a McDonald's gift certificate, you can assume that the giver of the leather jacket is more serious about you than the other guy. Most boys use gifts as a way to explain how they feel, since words can be more difficult. On the flip side, the more expensive the gift, the more demands will be made of you. Once you accept the leather jacket, that person may expect you to hold hands in public, talk to him on the phone all hours of the night, or tell other guys that you're unavailable. Expensive gifts come with strings.

MY TESTIMONY

I received a ring with three diamonds on it when I was a junior in high school. I never heard of girls getting any kind of ring besides a friendship ring or an engagement ring. I wasn't crazy about the guy who gave me the ring, and I definitely wasn't serious about him. So, when he gave it to me, I was completely shocked. At his urging, I put the ring on, and I thought it looked nice, but I told him that I felt that it was too expensive and I wasn't ready to think about a serious, serious relationship. I was just dating, and that ring was taking me places that I didn't want to go. He refused to take the ring back to the store and gave it to one of my friends to hold for me, since I wouldn't take it from him directly. We didn't continue dating because, as I had figured, the ring symbolized a serious relationship, and I knew that I wasn't ready to have one.

BLUEPRINT

I will not accept a gift unless I'm willing to accept the demands of the gift as well.

YOUR TESTIMONY

What types of gifts do you think are too much?

There is so much on television about plastic surgery—women getting nose jobs or breast implants. And in the magazines every other model or celebrity is described as having a weave. How am I supposed to keep up with all of this?

---

rule 17

Just because you don't have breast implants, a weave, or colored contacts doesn't mean that you won't get a date.

The images we see on television and in magazines and movies suggest that we have to look a certain way in order to be likeable, successful, and in a relationship. But those so-called "perfect" images, much like the medium they come from, are fake and unattainable. Every girl is not going to have breast implants, long wavy hair, and exotically colored eyes. And that's okay. There seems to be a growing number of guys who only want girls who look like they stepped out of a hip-hop video. But there are plenty more who want a girl who stands out naturally and who isn't a clone of every other person they've ever seen.

MY TESTIMONY

Teenagers are getting nose jobs and breast implants as sweet-sixteen birthday presents. Weaves are as commonplace as shampoo. And colored contacts have become so commonplace, it's not a question of do you have them, but what color are you wearing today? When I was growing up, "good hair" grew from the scalp, and "hair weave" was a dirty little word. But in this era of liberated and adjustable beauty, we still have to be sure that these additions to our physical self are not subtracting from our emotional self. Whether you look like Beyoncé or not, be comfortable with what you look like. No matter how you appear, there is somebody out there who is going to love you for you.

BLUEPRINT

If I decide to alter my look, that's my choice. But I'm not going to feel pressured to do so.

YOUR TESTIMONY

I think plastic surgery is . . .

My best friend's old boyfriend hit on me when I saw him recently.
My best friend says she doesn't like him anymore. Should I date him?

———

rule 18

You shouldn't date your best friend's ex-boyfriend.

*I*t happens all the time. You see it on TV every week. A girl breaks up with her boyfriend and proclaims to the world that she doesn't want him anymore. Then, before her announcement can travel through the neighborhood, her best friend has hooked up with him. In Hollywood these stories typically have a happy ending, but in the real world, feelings are involved, friendships end, and somebody always ends up crying. A girl who says she doesn't care about her ex-boyfriend might be telling the truth, but she might be in denial or preventing you from knowing how she feels. There are a small number of cases where a girl may not mind her best friend dating her ex-boyfriend, but in most cases it will bother her. Wouldn't you rather keep the best friend and play it safe? After all, he's not the only boy in the school or in the world.

MY TESTIMONY

Amongst my close-knit crew, we never dated each other's ex-boyfriends. That was a line that we didn't cross. At one of our sleepovers, I remember us talking about that. Lizette raised the point, "When somebody says that they're over a boyfriend, sometimes they really aren't." Where were we coming from, that was the whole point. If feelings are still there between your best friend and her ex, you don't want to be caught in the middle. And there's never absolute proof that all of the feelings are dead. A girl I used to be close to told me five years after the fact that she dated one of my ex-boyfriends. I couldn't believe it. She and I were best friends in eighth, ninth, and tenth grade, and now she was telling me that after high school she had dated my ex. I recall conversations when we said that we could never do that to each other, and yet she did it. I lost a sense of trust that I had with her when she told me about their relationship. I no longer had feelings for the guy, but because she had told me that she would never date one of my ex-boyfriends and she did anyway, that kinda makes her a liar.

BLUEPRINT

I will not allow a boy to break up my relationship with my best friend.

YOUR TESTIMONY

What are the real reasons you wouldn't date your best friend's boyfriend?

There's a boy I know who is really sweet. He's asked me out a few times, but I've said no because he's not that cute. I'm afraid my friends will tease me for dating an ugly guy. Should I date him anyway?

---

rule 19

Consider dating guys who aren't cute.

*M*ost girls have heard the phrase that looks are only skin deep, but they don't really understand what it means. A good-looking guy could be hateful deep inside and not treat you well. Yet a guy who is unattractive on the surface may be a sweetheart underneath. Our society encourages us to worship beauty and neglect uplifting values. Yet when you're in a relationship with someone, you'll quickly learn how ugly his personality can make him. Wouldn't it be better to date someone with basic looks who treats you well than someone who looks like a model and treats you like trash?

MY TESTIMONY

Bryce wasn't the most attractive person that I'd ever seen. He would have never won a "Best-Looking" contest in high school. When we first met, the idea of a date never entered my mind. He was friends with one of my college classmates, and he seemed like a nice enough person. He begged the friend who introduced us to put in a good word for him so that I would agree to at least give him my phone number. After two months of totally ignoring Bryce, I finally went out on a date with him. To my complete surprise, he was a funny, spontaneous, intelligent, and easygoing person. Of all my college dating experiences, my relationship with Bryce was one of the most memorable. It's unfortunate that we live in a society where exterior looks prevent us from getting to know new people. I'm actually glad that Bryce didn't abandon the idea of dating me after two solid months of me saying "I told you, I'm not interested."

BLUEPRINT

The content of a young man's character is more important than his looks.

YOUR TESTIMONY

I never considered talking to _____, but now I think he . . .

Is the guy I've spent all night talking to at a party really a stranger?

---

rule 20

Don't ride home from a party with an unfamiliar person.

$\mathcal{I}$n elementary school we were all told not to talk to or go anywhere with strangers. In fact, most of us were specifically instructed to notify an authority figure if a stranger approached us at all. However, with age comes confidence, and we begin to see people who we don't know as nonthreatening. We let our defenses down and unwittingly put ourselves in danger. A person that you just met at a club is still a stranger. You don't know him. Many girls go missing every year because they let their guard down. Just because you don't know anyone who has been abused, raped, or murdered by a stranger doesn't mean it can't happen to you.

MY TESTIMONY

Colleges are known for good parties. When I was in school, it was nothing to see Jam Master Jay or Kid Capri chillin' at the party. One Friday night, my friend Elise and I went to the club, danced, met new guys, and had a wonderful time. We always said that we'd stick together when we went out, but this guy from Ohio had her trippin'. She left me on the dance floor and said, "I'm riding home with Jabari." I pulled her arm and told her not to go, but she said that she was really feelin' him. When I got back to our house, Elise wasn't there yet. All night I wondered if she was okay. Jabari seemed cool, but we didn't know him. The next morning she came home and told me that Jabari was wack. After she refused to have sex with him, he wouldn't let her use the phone or bring her home until the morning. Since her place was too far to walk, she slept sitting in a corner on the floor. Needless to say, Elise was mad when I saw her that morning. She didn't fully understand that she should have been grateful that she made it home at all.

BLUEPRINT

I will not endanger my life by putting it in the care of a stranger.

YOUR TESTIMONY

What type of information do you know about a friend that you couldn't possibly know about a stranger?

I met a guy in a teen chat room,
and he seems really cool.
Should I meet him in person?

---

rule **21**

Cyberdating is here, but you still have to be sensible.

*W*ith the popularity of the Internet, meeting people online is easy. Skeptics say cyberspace is no place to find a date. Internet zealots say cyberdating is as revolutionary for dating as the advent of the telephone. Reality is somewhere in between those two extremes. When chatting with strangers on the Internet, exercise caution. Remember that you've never seen them, you don't know their friends, and you don't know where they live. And everything that they type to you in an instant message could very well be a lie. For all intents and purposes, your Internet boyfriend could be a fifty-five-year-old convicted pedophile. Then again, he could be who he says he is. Use your brain every time you sign on. This means don't agree to meet with anyone from the Internet by yourself, show some of the e-mail messages to a responsible adult, allow an adult to coordinate any offline date, and report any offensive e-mails to the proper authorities.

MY TESTIMONY

I recently learned of a college student who began an Internet relationship. She was so interested in taking the relationship to the next level, she ventured to Michigan without her parents' knowledge. Her "boyfriend" was exactly who he said he was. She wasn't hurt in her visit, wasn't raped, and wasn't mistreated. But she could have been. When she left her dorm for the weekend trip to Michigan, she didn't tell anyone but her roommate. Had anything gone wrong, only her roommate would have been able to supply minimal information regarding the Internet boyfriend. If she had not safely returned from her trip, her parents would not have been able to accept or explain her actions. That's something worth thinking about.

BLUEPRINT

I will engage in safe practices if I elect to cyberdate.

YOUR TESTIMONY

My experience in chatting on the Internet has been . . .

People spend a lot of time judging girls by what they wear. If it's what's inside that counts, why can't I wear whatever I want?

rule 22

You will be judged by your appearance.

*I*t's been said a million times, "What's on the inside is what counts." Character, integrity, and trustworthiness are all qualities that reside within a person. However, when initially meeting somebody, it's difficult to get past what they're wearing and what they look like. Clothes and personal grooming speak volumes about the kind of people that we are. A shirt that says "I love boys" makes a different statement than a shirt that has "Hip Hop Forever" inscribed on it. A pierced tongue conveys a sentiment different from the one expressed by a pierced earlobe. And hair that looks unsightly sends a different message than hair that was recently combed. We should always we aware of our personal appearance and be willing to accept what it is saying about who we are.

MY TESTIMONY

They were called "hot pants" in the seventies, "Daisy Dukes" in the nineties, and today they're short shorts. Outfits that are super short convey sexiness, looseness, and provocativeness even when that's not the wearer's intention. I loved my faded blue Daisy Dukes. I wore them with a white short-sleeved turtleneck sweater, a reddish brown suede belt, and matching strapped sandals. Whenever I put this outfit on, I felt like I was on top of the world. I felt this outfit accentuated my physique. One day I was walking through the mall in my Daisy Dukes, and guys kept turning their heads, looking at me like I was a piece of meat. I didn't enjoy the kind of attention that I received while wearing those shorts. After that experience in the mall, I cut back on wearing my Daisy Dukes. I believe that people should be able to feel comfortable in what they are wearing, but others' actions will make you uncomfortable. One of our greatest challenges as women is balancing the idea of freedom with making good choices.

BLUEPRINT

I will be cognizant of how my appearance may be viewed by others.

YOUR TESTIMONY

When I was wearing _____, it seemed that . . .

Football, basketball, baseball?
I can't follow any of it.
Why do guys love sports so much,
anyway?

---

rule 23

Do yourself a favor: learn a little about sports.

*M*ost guys love sports. They can rattle off athletes' statistics faster than their own mothers' birthdays. Male athletes and nonathletes alike have affinity for basketballs, footballs, baseballs, and so on. A young lady wanting to have a conversation with a new guy will find that sports will almost always be a hit. Young men are impressed when a girl knows terms like "offensive foul," "ERA," and "illegal defense." Learning something about sports will allow you to have something else in common with your potential boyfriend.

MY TESTIMONY

When I was growing up in a basketball-loving household, the NBA All-Star weekend was an annual ritual. As a young person I watched sports with my father and brother. When I went to college and moved out on my own, professional sports was still of big interest to me. On one of my first dates with Marcus, we watched the NBA's slam dunk contest. Marcus thought that we'd watch a movie after dinner. He was surprised when I said, "Either we're watching the slam dunk contest, or I'm going home." The look on his face was of shock and satisfaction. He couldn't believe he'd met someone who enjoyed basketball like he did, but he was sure glad that he had.

BLUEPRINT

I can utilize sports knowledge as a unique bridge of communication and discussion when I am attempting to break the ice.

YOUR TESTIMONY

Next time there's a big game on television, watch it and make a list of the things you enjoyed. The list might be longer than you think.

*Are some guys simply destined
to be just your friend?*

---

rule 24

Some dates aren't meant to become boyfriends.

*I*t's important to realize that every boy you date isn't supposed to become your boyfriend. Some will leave an imprint on your heart and mind forever. But some you won't remember past high school graduation. Some guys are better left unmet. Many girls journey through their middle and high school years snagging as many dates as possible. But toward the end of their senior years, they're drained, exploited, and often left feeling unloved. Dating is an opportunity to get to know somebody, but be careful about how much of yourself you release. Once you let it go, it's hard to get it back. And not everyone is worthy of you.

MY TESTIMONY

Greek weekend in Virginia Beach was the college party of all parties—a dating smorgasbord. Young African-American adults from all over traveled to the beach on Labor Day weekend with the sole purpose of finding new people to hook up with. In a weekend, you could easily meet fifty or more guys. Some were cute, and others weren't. Some of them had game; others could hardly speak intelligible English. Of all the guys that I and my friends met on Labor Day weekends, not one became a boyfriend. They were nice to talk to for seventy-two hours, but after that, there was really no connection. The guys just left that kind of impression.

BLUEPRINT

I will not force myself to make every date become a boyfriend.

YOUR TESTIMONY

I wish I hadn't dated _____ because . . .

A guy just tried to grope me in the hallway. My friend says he likes me; I think he disrespected me. Why do guys do that, and what should I do?

---

rule 25

Own your body and stand up for your rights.

S ome people still believe that women are less significant than men, and can therefore be beaten, groped, verbally abused, raped, and underpaid without consequence. Knowing this attitude toward women, girls must realize that they are often in harm's way by their very existence. Girls must resist being in dangerous places or associating with people who are violent and disrespectful toward women. Only by protecting ourselves and informing men of how we want to be treated will we ever change the treatment of women and girls.

MY TESTIMONY

The spaces at a club, in a basketball gymnasium, or in a hallway are often tight. So cluttered, in fact, that through my life I've always been watchful of who I'm standing next to or who is nearby. As we walked through a club, on our way to a table, a strange male felt my friend Gina's behind. I was standing several paces behind Gina, and I looked this guy directly in the face. Before I could say anything, Gina leaned back and "accidentally" spilled her drink on his shirt. She sarcastically said, "My fault," but we all knew she spilled her drink on him in retaliation for touching her inappropriately. As he grimaced, looking at his crisp silk shirt, we kept going and sat down. Though retaliation isn't always a good idea in dealing with disrespectful men, I bet the guy in the club thought twice before he reached out to touch anybody else's behind that night.

BLUEPRINT

I will not allow myself to be inappropriately touched or mistreated by males.

YOUR TESTIMONY

I witnessed a girl being treated unfairly when . . .

My girlfriend and I both like the same guy, but I don't want to compete with her for him. Our friendship is too important. What should we do?

---

rule 26

Two best friends can both like the same guy.

*J*f two friends meet a guy at the same time, it's highly possible that they'll both be attracted to him. Instead of arguing over who should date him, perhaps jumping double dutch or flipping a coin would be better. Then the lucky winner gets to pursue the guy with no regrets or hesitations. No friendships are devastated, and feelings shouldn't really be hurt.

MY TESTIMONY

Among my crew, we never were attracted to the same kind of guys. Our tastes were so different. If one of us liked an athletic guy, another one of us was attracted to a square guy, or another liked a hustler-type guy. But from our experiences and having other acquaintances in school, we knew that friendships had been destroyed over guys. Girls in our school had stopped speaking to one another because they liked the same person. Best friends had stopped associating because a guy gave both friends his phone number. In these situations, where friendships were terminated because of potential boyfriends, I can guarantee that neither girl is with the guy today. And, what's worse, the girls don't have each other either.

BLUEPRINT

I will remember the importance of friendship if me and one of my friends ever likes the same guy.

YOUR TESTIMONY

If me and my best friend liked the same person, I would . . .

Hey, dating is about experience, right?
So shouldn't a girl try to date as many
guys as possible?

_____

rule 27

You shouldn't pursue every guy that you see.

There are a whole lot of fish in the sea, but everyone doesn't have to have your phone number. Guys are taught "the more, the better" in obtaining girlfriends, but the same philosophy isn't fit for girls. Most girls emotionally attach themselves to a mate much faster than guys, and consequently get hurt more when the union doesn't last.

MY TESTIMONY

If a guy made eye contact with Tanisha on campus, she would consider hooking up with him. First, there was eye contact, and then she wanted to know if we thought he liked her. Tanisha spent hours evaluating the potential of relationships, and wondering if there were unspoken meanings in everything from a handshake to a leg twitch. But of all the guys that Tanisha chased, 50 percent were already in a relationship, 25 percent just weren't interested, and another 15 percent weren't worth anyone's time. It goes to show that of the ten guys that you meet on any one day, it's likely only one is worth your time or energy.

BLUEPRINT

I am not in any contest to obtain phone numbers or dates.

YOUR TESTIMONY

I thought about talking to _____, but then I decided not to because . . .

Will a bad boy ever change?
Sometimes they just need the right girl
to come along, right?

———————

rule 28

Most bad boys won't reform.

a guy you used to like in the seventh grade was recently released from juvenile hall after serving a stint for shoplifting. You love his thug persona. He appears to fear nothing and nobody. But he still talks about boosting items from department stores and smoking joints on the corner. You're concerned that he may still be doing bad things when he's not around you. And you should be concerned. Most people can't escape old habits. If you don't want to be a part of that lifestyle, stay away from dating guys in it.

MY TESTIMONY

"Growing up poor is hard," Nadia's boyfriend, David, would often say. "Even when I want to do right, there's someone trying to get me to do wrong." Every time he left the house, he told us, there were at least seven ways to distract him from going to school. It was like devils on the block enticing him into mischief. In his early teen years, David got into a lot of trouble, but when he hooked up with Nadia, we thought he'd changed. Nadia prayed for David and loved him like no other. When rumors started circulating that he was robbing people at gunpoint, she didn't believe it. People started telling our whole crew that he was a stick-up man. After three years of dating, Nadia turned on the eleven-o'clock news one night and saw a videotape of David robbing a convenience store. When she saw him on the news, she told me she couldn't believe her eyes. It was like the person she thought she loved didn't exist. I remember her talking about how everybody was warning her, but she just thought they were trying to ruin her relationship with David.

BLUEPRINT

I will not ignore the dangerous lifestyle choices my potential boyfriend makes. That lifestyle is not suitable for me.

YOUR TESTIMONY

I noticed _____'s bad-boy ways when . . .

People put so much stock in first impressions. Do they really matter that much?

---

rule 29

First impressions make a difference.

*W*hatever crosses your mind when you see somebody for the first time, that image is likely to stick with you. If you recently met somebody, and his eyes were bloodshot and swollen at that initial encounter, you will probably think that he was high and that he's high all the time. It doesn't matter if you see him fifty more times without his eyes being swollen; you're still likely to remember that first impression. So when you go out and know that you'll be meeting people for the first time, you have to consider how you're going to present yourself. What impression do you want to leave people with? Don't assume that anyone can see past what is displayed on the outside.

MY TESTIMONY

When I was called to interview a famous rap star prior to a

concert in the late nineties, I knew that I had to present myself in a certain manner. I selected my wardrobe with professionalism, trustworthiness, and respect in mind. As I walked into the star's dressing room and saw scantily clad women in bra tops and thong-revealing super-short minis, I was glad for my basic T-shirt and jeans. I didn't get mistaken for a groupie. When I saw the girls licking their lips in the backstage hallway, I was happy to have my pen, pad, and tape recorder so that I wouldn't be taken for anything less than a person conducting business. I could have chosen to look like a groupie, but that's not the impression that I wanted to leave anybody that I met backstage.

BLUEPRINT

I will present myself in the manner in which I want to be remembered and recognized.

YOUR TESTIMONY

If I could go back in time and change history, it would be the first time that I met . . .

A girl in the neighborhood was recently assaulted. How do I avoid becoming a victim?

---

rule 30

Always pay attention to your surroundings.

We shouldn't have to worry about becoming victims of rape or murder. There should be enough laws and law enforcement to protect us. Unfortunately, our world is not perfect, and we have to engage in precautions for our own safety.

MY TESTIMONY

In 2002, there was a stretch of parking-lot rapes in the suburbs of Washington, D.C. Since I live in that area, I was very concerned. The victims were young women who were walking alone. When the 2001 Chandra Levy case broke, it was revealed that women joggers in Rock Creek Park had been murdered over a period of time. Young women are often the target of predators. When we're in the mall, we have to be aware if we're being followed. We have to stop and look around. We need to carry Mace and know how to use it. Self-defense should be a mandatory life course, just like English is to college freshmen. Above all, we must be watchful of where we are and who is nearby. Our lives are depending on it.

BLUEPRINT

Knowing what and who is around me will reduce my chances of becoming a victim.

YOUR TESTIMONY

Make a list of ways that you can start being more safe. Congratulate yourself each time you realize that you're creating safer habits.

PHASE 2

Relationships

An emotional connection, a desire to be attached, or a craving for partnership encourages people to enter into relationships. When based on a strong foundation, relationships can flourish. But there are many kinds of relationships, and we each have our own idea of what type of union we want. Before you enter into any relationship, know what you want out of it.

What makes a guy your boyfriend, as opposed to simply a guy you're dating?

---

rule 31

Relationships mean different things to different people.

When two people decide to have a relationship, their attitudes, definitions, and expectations of relationships all come into play. For some, an exclusive relationship connotes a sexual one. For others it means a platonic commitment. Some relationships are stagnant, while others grow through different stages and meet specific goals. Going with someone might mean, "You have to be my prom date," or it might mean, "I'm the only one that can take you to the movies." Before you decide to partner with another, you should find out what "relationship" means to the other person.

MY TESTIMONY

Brian believed that he could date a girl and expect her to have sex with him, but yet not be considered her boyfriend. He felt that girls should be ready and willing to have intimate relations without a commitment. As a college senior, I hadn't seriously considered that perspective before. Was I living in the dark ages? In this case, how would you know that you were even in a relationship? I quickly realized that I didn't have time for a person like Brian in my life. It was obvious that he didn't understand my thoughts on intimacy, and he wouldn't understand Partnership 101 if it was taught by a relationship therapist.

BLUEPRINT

In any relationship that I enter into, I will strive to understand the other person's expectations.

YOUR TESTIMONY

List what type of things you expect from a boyfriend. What type of things might he expect from you?

My boyfriend has a bad temper, and once he punched me. Afterward he was really sorry and promised never to do it again, but some days his temper scares me. Should I stay with him?

---

rule 32

A boyfriend that hits you isn't worth keeping.

*L*ove isn't supposed to physically hurt. It's really that simple. The two of you can scream, yell, and disagree. If you can't resolve an issue, walk away to cool off or to regain your composure. The key to a successful relationship is communicating. You can't communicate with clenched fists, blackened eyes, and busted lips.

MY TESTIMONY

One slap across the face is all it took for me to realize that I was in a relationship with the wrong person. An argument about who was going to drive to the football game, and *bam*—one slap across the face. Initially, I was more shocked than anything. It was like a movie of someone else's life, and I was watching it. Except the stinging underneath my skin wasn't make-believe. It was as real as the teardrops and as real as the conversations that I had terminating that relationship. See ya!

BLUEPRINT

Physical abuse does not have a place in any relationship of mine.

YOUR TESTIMONY

If I was ever physically abused in a relationship, I would . . .

I want to get my boyfriend's name tattooed on my arm, but my mom went off when I told her. I don't understand why she's trippin'. He and I are going to be together forever.

---

rule 33

Boyfriend name tattoos will probably last longer than the relationship.

*Y*ou're not the first one to think that the ultimate statement of love or commitment is to have your boyfriend's name tattooed somewhere on your body. In fact, it would be a great idea, if relationships lasted forever. But most of them don't. So if you decide to get his name tattooed, don't forget about the long list of people who've had to figure out a way to remove the lasting ink when the relationship was long since over. Do you really want to be another one of those people?

MY TESTIMONY

Lisa has Jamon's name tattooed on her wrist. It's slightly above the place where her watch rests. She dated Jamon for about three years before getting the tattoo. As a statement of their love, they each were tattooed with the other's name. About eighteen months after their love has simmered down and the relationship has puttered out, Lisa still has Jamon's name on her wrist. She maintains, "It's not that bad, you can hardly see it when I'm wearing my bracelets." Yeah, that's true, but "hardly" doesn't cut it. The reality is that every day Lisa has the name of a guy she no longer can even stand tattooed on her wrist.

BLUEPRINT

If I decide to get a name tattooed on my body, I will make sure it's a name worthy of marking my body for the rest of my life. After all, my body is a temple.

YOUR TESTIMONY

I thought about getting a tattoo. This is what I think . . .

I have trouble talking to my boyfriend about certain things. I don't think he'll understand. So our relationship isn't the way that I want it to be.

---

rule 34

Communication and listening are your greatest assets in any relationship.

Communication is the key to letting your partner know what you want out of any relationship. Many of us remain tight-lipped when we encounter a problem and quietly hope that the other party will figure it out. Most times they never do. It's our responsibility to inform someone of our viewpoints. And on the other hand, we must develop our ability to listen so that we understand our partner's personality, needs, desires, and feelings. Listening allows you to better relate to his situation and structure your conversations accordingly. Remember, the basis of any relationship is your ability to communicate and listen.

MY TESTIMONY

My friend Paula has always been able to get guys to do anything she requests. They could be platonic friends that are boys or actual boyfriends, it doesn't matter; she has a powerful way to communicate. I used to sit on the couch and listen to her phone conversations. She seemed to be so attuned to whatever emotional situation her boyfriends were going through. Once when I was in college, I asked her for a couple hundred dollars to help out a friend. She didn't have the money, and neither did I, and I wasn't going to ask my parents for it. I called Paula and explained the scenario. Within three hours she had one of her "big brothers" wire me the money. When I asked her how she was able to do it, she explained that she let him know that a friend of a friend was in crisis. The way that she explained it, she had connected with her big brother's need to assist people in need.

BLUEPRINT

I must communicate so that I can effectively relate to people.

YOUR TESTIMONY

_____ *doesn't understand my thoughts on . . . I need to talk about . . .*

My boyfriend's ex-girlfriend keeps saying
that she wants to meet with me.
Do you think I should?

---

rule 35

Leave ex-girlfriends out of the picture.

*I*n prehistoric societies cavemen probably clubbed each other in fights for their woman's loyalty. In today's more sophisticated society, relationships should be a nonconfrontational matter of choice. Ex-boyfriends and ex-girlfriends need to mind their own business. It's unfortunate that jealousy, envy, and plain stupidity lead people to interfere in situations where they don't belong. If you're ever approached by an ex-girlfriend, remember that your relationship is only between two people, and the ex-girl ain't one of them.

MY TESTIMONY

I was dating Londell in my junior year of high school. After a football game, me and my friends Rayna and Mika were followed by Londell's ex-girlfriend. As we walked toward the parking lot, waiting for Londell to change out of his football uniform, the ex-girlfriend was just staring at us and then looking at the ground. She never said anything to us directly, but every time we took ten steps forward, she took five. It seemed that she was stalking us. When Londell finally came out of the building, she called his name and was ignored. As we all kept walking, she continued to follow behind us. When we got in the car and drove away, there she stood, wide-eyed, looking as if she had lost her best friend and her mind. As I rode home I couldn't figure out why Londell's ex-girlfriend was following us.

BLUEPRINT

Ex-girlfriends do not have a place in my current relationship.

YOUR TESTIMONY

List three things you can focus on when your relationship is over: _____, _____, _____.

I don't understand how it is that I can be crazy about someone for three months and then not be interested. Is there something wrong with me?

---

rule 36

Feelings change.

*O*ver time, your emotions will intensify or lessen. Nothing remains the same. You can look at it as a kindness that has been bestowed on all of humanity. In most cases this happens because your needs in the relationship have changed, or you've seen a side of your partner that you didn't know existed. Always embrace change in your relationship, because nothing in life remains stagnant. Remember, change is a sign of growth.

MY TESTIMONY

Gina used to think Flex was the best guy in the world. The star player on his basketball team, he had light eyes and a nice smile. In fact, while everyone else was breaking out in pimples, Flex's skin remained smooth and flawless. Our group of friends thought Flex was all right, but we were not about to start his fan club. He was always ditching Gina on dates, giving her the cheapest gifts on any holiday, and talking primarily about himself in every conversation. He was annoying, to say the least, but Gina never thought so. Then one day, after waiting for him at his house for five hours—where he never showed up—Gina stopped liking Flex so much. She stopped wanting his hand-me-down affections. And just like that, she was over Flex.

BLUEPRINT

I will accept my feelings changing as yet another aspect into my growth as a young lady.

YOUR TESTIMONY

I used to feel a certain way about _____. But now I feel . . .

What exactly
is female intuition?

rule 37

Female intuition increases your sensibilities.

*a*re there times when you feel uncomfortable about something, but you can't put your finger on why? Perhaps it was a reference made during a conversation or a gesture that you witnessed out in public—something rang a warning bell in your mind. Most women have a unique sense of intuition. It prevents them from being hurt, embarrassed, and in some cases traumatized. In relationships, intuition should be appreciated and utilized as a compass in our journey. When the alarm of your intuition sounds, listen to it. Conduct an investigation until the alarm goes off. Your intuition may be telling you to watch out for your mate.

MY TESTIMONY

Half the time I called Will, he'd have to call me back. The

other half, I would hear other girls' voices in the background. Will would always say it was his cousin or his cousin's friends. When I first told my friends about it, we didn't focus on it. But after a couple of months, I started thinking that Will had another girl on the side. One day me and my friends called Will from a pay phone. We were about five minutes from his house. Again, he said that he had to call me back. When I showed up at his house to surprise him, he had another girl sitting on the couch, and his cousin was nowhere to be found. It was the girl that he'd told me that he was no longer dating.

BLUEPRINT

God gave me intuition for a reason. I will listen to it.

YOUR TESTIMONY

Have you ever ignored your intuition? Did your intuition turn out to be right?

*I don't know what it is about him,
but I just can't stand my best friend's
new boyfriend. Should I tell her?*

---

rule 38

Friends shouldn't dog each other's boyfriends.

Your favorite color is red, your best friend's favorite is purple. She likes chicken soft tacos, you like beef-filled enchiladas. She has a boyfriend who she's crazy about, and you think her guy is sneaky and kinda scary looking. In all other cases, you and your best friend can agree to disagree, but with her boyfriend, you won't say anything nice about him. If you can overlook her choice of taco, why not the boyfriend? There's not enough paper in the world to write the name of every girl who has lost a friend because of saying negative things about her boyfriend. Your friendships with your best friends are more important than your opinion of their boyfriends.

MY TESTIMONY

I used to talk about Gina's boyfriend Flex all the time. To me he was snakelike, conniving, and always looked like he was trying to hide something. Whenever Gina brought him up, I had a negative comment. After a while Gina didn't want to talk to me about Flex because she knew that I wouldn't have anything positive to say. She knew that no matter how good he seemed to her, I refused to see any good in him. My relationship with Gina became strained during her Flex days, and it was all because I criticized her boyfriend every chance I got. It took me a long time to realize that it wasn't my purpose in life to bad-mouth Flex. One day I understood that I wouldn't want my girlfriends dogging the person that I was with, so I just stopped disparaging Flex.

BLUEPRINT

I will not say hurtful things about my friend's boyfriend just because I don't like him.

YOUR TESTIMONY

I don't like _____, but I'm not gonna talk about him. This is why I don't like him . . .

My boyfriend and I argue all the time.

Does that mean we should break up?

---

rule 39

Arguments are contests of intellect, will, and character.

*a*rguments may seem like nit-picking or aggravating discussions about nothing, but in a relationship, arguments reveal intelligence, personality, and the determination of both parties. In fact, most people will disguise their opinions, but in a heated argument their emotions will reveal their truths. Instead of viewing arguments as irrelevant, we should value them as necessary fact-finding missions that can inform and educate us about our partner.

MY TESTIMONY

Me and Bobby used to argue all the time. We fought about his fraternity, the sorority sister hangers-on, the type of world that we live in, and our school itself. Through our debates, I learned that he felt hazing was a part of being in a fraternity, that sister sorors could be a good source of support, and that education reform for inner-city kids would always be in his belief system. Besides learning about our relationship, I discovered the kind of man that Bobby was becoming. Even in our most heated exchanges, I could respect the man and gain unexpected insight. I wish every argument that I had in life was as informative as the ones I had with Bobby.

BLUEPRINT

There is something to be learned in every argument that I have.

YOUR TESTIMONY

Make a list of some things you learned from a recent argument.

My boyfriend hates my best friend.
It's gotten to the point where I can't spend
time with them both. What should I do?

_____

rule 40

Just because two people love you doesn't mean they will love each other.

We can't all get along like the members of Destiny's Child. The rest of us must accept personality, attitude, and social differences. In an ideal world, a guy, a girl, and their best friends would all get along. But that is hardly ever the case. There's no reason that the boyfriend has to attend everything that the girls do together. And the best friend doesn't have to be involved in everything that the couple does. Keeping the boyfriend and the best friend on separate but equal terms can keep everybody happy.

MY TESTIMONY:

When I dated Bobby, he didn't have just one best friend, he

had several of them. Our relationship got serious shortly after he pledged to a college fraternity, and when his frat brothers found out he had a girlfriend, it was like they all had something against me. When I visited with Bobby at the house, there was always this unwelcoming feeling that came from several of the other guys. Even though Bobby had invited me to the house, they seemed to grunt when I rang the doorbell. I started complaining to Bobby about it, and he felt that I was overreacting. Just the same, though, I was reluctant to visit Bobby at the frat house. For the most part, he wouldn't agree with me that they had something against me, but we agreed that when we did hook up, it would be at my place and not his. In that case, I guess he was trying to keep his girlfriend from all of his best friends.

BLUEPRINT

My best friend and my boyfriend can peacefully exist, even if it's separately.

YOUR TESTIMONY

My best friend and my boyfriend get along or don't get along because . . .

My boyfriend just dumped me,
and I'm devastated! He already has
a new girlfriend.

———————

rule 41

You may get dumped
for another chick.

He'll say, "We need time apart," or "I don't think I'm ready to have a girlfriend right now." Then five days later, you see him kissing another girl in the hallway and holding her hand. You're right to be angry, disappointed, and upset. But only for a short while. The upside to this scenario is as follows: (1) The guy respected you enough not to two-time you. (2) If the relationship had remained, you would have wondered why he wasn't in love with you. (3) You're one step closer to meeting your true love.

MY TESTIMONY

Niecey didn't think any guy in the world could compare to Rich. If he was going to be at a basketball game, we'd have to be there. If he was going to the bowling alley, we were standing in the parking lot waiting for him to arrive. He wasn't even cute—in fact, he looked like a weather-beaten tree with eyes and a haircut. Niecey and Rich had been dating for several months when all of a sudden Rich ended their relationship. He told her that he didn't want to be in a relationship anymore, and that he needed space to breathe. Two days later, Niecey and I went to the movies to try to lift her spirits. To our complete disgust, we saw Rich in the last row kissing this girl so hard that we don't know how he was still breathing. So much for him needing space to breathe.

BLUEPRINT

If my boyfriend ever chooses another girl over me, it is no reflection on who I am or who I will become.

YOUR TESTIMONY

When _____ broke up the relationship, I felt . . .

Can a breakup ever be mutual?

---

rule 42

Relationships can end on good terms.

*I*t takes mature people to remain friendly after their relationship has ended. They realize that some unions aren't meant to be, and there's no need for anger or hate. Some individuals are big enough to see that the end of one aspect of their lives could signal the beginning of another more fulfilling part. Honesty, sensitivity, and communication are all vital in being cool with your boyfriend after the relationship is over.

MY TESTIMONY

I met Gary at a college basketball game. I bumped into him trying to get to a concession stand. He stood about six-one, and when I looked up at him, he seemed to have a glow illuminating his body. We talked for a few minutes, exchanged numbers and promised that we would call each other. We didn't. But three weeks later at a college party, we saw each other and embraced like we were long-lost buddies. We eventually started a relationship and had so much fun getting to know each other. Gary knew how to laugh and didn't believe in having bad days. When our relationship didn't work out, we moved on and had no regrets. I sent him a "breakup letter," and he called me and complimented me on how well it was written. We both laughed, and then the relationship was over.

BLUEPRINT

Being sensitive to my partner's feelings will assist me in leaving the relationship on a positive note.

YOUR TESTIMONY

I can leave this relationship on good terms by . . .

My girlfriend says that you should jump right back into dating after a relationship ends. What do you think?

---

rule 43

Chill-out time is necessary in between each relationship.

When a relationship ends, it takes time to resolve emotions and figure out how to proceed in the next phase of your life. Unions are not made overnight, and so feelings do not disappear overnight. When hearts are shattered, time is necessary to heal them. Rushing from one relationship to the next prevents the evaluation and restoration processes from starting.

MY TESTIMONY

After Londell and I broke up, I probably shouldn't have dated for a while. But I did, and I picked people who I wouldn't have considered if I was not still emotionally vulnerable. I dated people who were weak-minded, unintelligent, closeted homosexuals, street hustlers, and secret dope addicts. It was like I had to have a boyfriend, no matter how pathetic. Years later, I realized I didn't need a boyfriend; I needed to be by myself, to heal and make individual decisions for my own betterment. And until I allowed myself that space, I continued to hurt.

BLUEPRINT

It's okay to be single after one relationship has ended.

YOUR TESTIMONY

Now that the relationship with _____ *is over, I'm going to . . .*

*Sometimes I think my boyfriend
is lying to me.
Am I just jumping to conclusions?*

---

rule 44

Some lies are obvious.

*Y*ou don't have to be a cast member of *Law and Order* to know when somebody is lying to you. Some lies are so blatantly false that you can smell the polyurethane in the air. Our mind often refuses to accept what we don't believe is desirable. Often we make the mistake of believing only what we want to believe. Know this: a relationship built on deception and untruths is not gonna last. When we trick our brains into accepting things that are inaccurate, we are only delaying the inevitable—a broken heart.

MY TESTIMONY

Sitting on the porch at Niecey's house, Gina noticed a bruise on Flex's neck. "What's that?" she asked. Flex touched his neck and responded, "I'm always getting hurt in basketball practice." Gina said, "Oh, let me go get you some ice." When Gina left the room, Niecey and I looked at each other. That bruise was the biggest, most purple hickey we had ever seen. Months later, when Gina finally ended her relationship with Flex, she talked about all the times that she suspected that he had lied to her but ignored it. At this point, she had gotten over the desire for him to be her boyfriend and was tired of being treated like a fool.

BLUEPRINT

Accepting lies as truth can only hurt me.

YOUR TESTIMONY

I felt _____ was lying when . . .

Is there ever a situation
when you should fight over a guy?

---

rule 45

Never fight over a guy.

*N*othing is as ridiculous as two girls at a club taking their jewelry off and smearing Vaseline on their faces to fight over their so-called boyfriend. When the fight is in progress, the guy is standing there with his boys, laughing—laughing at two girls being immature. He's not thinking, "Whoever wins will be my girlfriend." He's thinking, "I can make girls do anything." When girls fight over boys, it gives too much power to the guys, and it gives the girls nothing.

MY TESTIMONY

I guess Lisa wanted to fight me when she realized that Londell had moved on to somebody else. She started calling my house to threaten me, playing on the phone, and following me in parking lots after football games. It was ridiculous. Whenever she did those things, I would tell Londell, and he would go off on her. I let him know that if Lisa ever said anything to me but "Hi," he'd wish he never met me. As for Lisa, just say we did fight. Okay, let's say I got a black eye, and she got a busted lip. What would happen then? I would still have left with the guy, so what would have been the point?

BLUEPRINT

I will not lower or disrespect myself by striking another girl over a guy.

YOUR TESTIMONY

I felt like fighting over _____ when . . .

What should I do if I find out
my best friend's boyfriend
is cheating on her?

---

rule 46

Knowing your best friend's boyfriend is a cheat is a problematic situation.

*Y*ou want to tell your best friend that you found out her boyfriend is a snake. You hate keeping secrets from your best friend. But on the other hand you don't want to be the person who reveals what a crab her boyfriend really is. Many good friendships are lost when a person gets in the middle of relationship business. You must weigh the entire situation before you decide to speak. If the infraction was minor, you might want to keep it to yourself. But if it was major—like him kissing another girl—get a witness, wait for it to happen again, and have another witness on hand. Then spill the beans to the girl-friend. In the end, you know that you were being a true friend, and someone else saw him being a cheat.

MY TESTIMONY

I've always been cool with all of my friend's boyfriends. I wasn't overly friendly, but I never made any of the guys feel that they had to impress me because they were dating one of my girls. Well, one somber day in my junior year of high school, Maya's boyfriend Andre called me. He told me that he was cheating on Maya with her pretend sister. I couldn't believe it. And I don't know why he called me. I'm not a shrink, and I wasn't holding a Catholic confessional. So there I was with this big secret that I knew would hurt my best friend. I had never really liked Andre—he was a shady character. But I loved Maya, and I wouldn't allow him to make a fool of her. So I met with Maya and told her. She probably didn't want to believe me, but she knew I'd never lie to her about anything like that. In the end, she dropped Andre and kicked her pretend sister to the curb.

BLUEPRINT

Being a good friend sometimes involves being the bearer of bad news.

YOUR TESTIMONY

If I ever found out about a girlfriend's boyfriend cheating, I would . . .

*My best friend never wants to talk
to me about my boyfriend.
It's like she's jealous or something.
Why can't she just be happy for me?*

---

rule 47

Most girls who don't have a boyfriend don't want to hear about yours.

When we think about people bragging, we usually associate it with people talking about their clothes, money, or cars that they have or what they are going to get. But bragging also applies to relationships. If you're constantly talking about your boyfriend (what you are planning to do together and the fun that you're having) to girls who don't have boyfriends, you're just being insensitive. Can you imagine Oprah going to a homeless woman and telling her about all the money she has? It's inconsiderate. You also have to be careful because when some people don't have what you have, they will stop at nothing to try to take it away from you.

MY TESTIMONY

I have to admit hearing Gina talk about her boyfriend all the time got on my nerves. She was always talking about what movie they saw, where they went, and what they did. I mean, I was ready to plug my ears. It wasn't that I was jealous that she had a boyfriend, I was just hoping that she could think of something else to talk about. Whenever I had a boyfriend, I tried hard not to talk about him incessantly. After twenty minutes on the phone talking about the same guy, did my girlfriends really want to hear more? I didn't think so.

BLUEPRINT

My boyfriend is not the center of my life. I have a lot to talk about besides him.

YOUR TESTIMONY

When I talked to _____ about my relationship, she seemed . . .

Sometimes my boyfriend says
little things that hurt my feelings.
Am I being too sensitive?

---

rule 48

People who claim to love you can use hurtful, demeaning comments in their conversations with you.

Some folks are brought up without any manners; others feel that being mean can get them what they want. And then there is another group of people who believe that they must put you down in order to feel good about themselves. It doesn't seem right, but the guy who says that he loves you more than anything in the world could be the same person throwing daggers at your self-confidence. A person who has to hurt your feelings and derail your self-esteem in his day-to-day conversation does not love you nearly as much as he says.

MY TESTIMONY

Bryce always had something negative to say about me. One day it'd be my hair: "You'd look better with longer hair." Another day it'd be my outfits: "So-and-so had the same kind of boots, but hers looked better than yours." No matter what I did, how I looked, or how I dressed, Bryce constantly had comments. And none of his comments were compliments. They were all criticisms. As I thought about his comments and looked at him, I remembered that he grew up being criticized for his looks and the clothes that he didn't have. He was talked about because he wasn't nearly as attractive as the other guys in his neighborhood, nor was he an athlete. When new fashions hit the stores, Bryce was never in line filling up his closet, so he carried that resentment from his childhood and hurled it onto the people closest to him. And unfortunately, for about fifteen months, it was me.

BLUEPRINT

I will not associate with people who claim to love me, but then try to hurt me with their put-downs and insults.

YOUR TESTIMONY

I was hurt when _____ said . . .

Is a monogamous relationship
really possible?

---

rule 49

A monogamous relationship means just you and your boyfriend.

*a*nybody can have a boyfriend or a girlfriend, but everybody isn't having one-on-one relationships. Some people know that they're not; others think that they are. When you enter into a romantic relationship, the terms should be defined. If it's a monogamous relationship, both you and your partner should abide by the rules. If you're having a relationship where you and your partner have people on the side, that information should be known by all parties. When people sneak around, telling lies and spreading germs, it leads to a big mess where a lot of feelings get hurt.

MY TESTIMONY

Many guys will tell you that they must be your one and only, and all the while they may have another chick on the side. Will told me again and again, "I better be your only one. I know you could only love me." For the first eleven months of the relationship, I actually believed that. Then I woke up and found out that Will had girls on the side throughout the entire time we dated. Clearly, he belonged in someone else's life.

BLUEPRINT

Any relationship that I enter into, I will know the guidelines and stick to them accordingly.

YOUR TESTIMONY

Does it seem that a lot of people don't want to have one-on-one relationships? Why or why not? What do you think of monogamous relationships?

*My boyfriend will make little comments
that tell me that he wants me to change.
Could this be a way for me to grow?*

---

rule 50

Always be yourself in every relationship.

*P*erhaps there's an attraction in pretending to be some-thing that we're not. Maybe an idea slips into our minds subconsciously—a feeling of not being satisfied with who we are. Not being comfortable in our own skin causes us to perform when we are around others. Just like actors playing a role, we hope that we'll be believed and loved in that role. But pretending is painful. Those who don't know that they're in a movie believe that they are falling for the real person when in fact that person is a fake. And the pre-tenders are scared as hell when the curtain comes down.

MY TESTIMONY

I remember one of my girlfriends saying that she would

never let a boyfriend see her without her makeup until after the wedding day. I laughed hard during that conversation. The thought of a groom not really knowing what his bride looked like was hilarious to me. But maybe I shouldn't have laughed so heartily. Sure, makeup is fine for what it does, but it should never replace who you are. Anyone who you are dating and who you believe cares about you should be able to see you as you really are and still love you anyway.

BLUEPRINT

I am who I am and what I am for a reason. I don't have to change to suit anyone's fancy but my own.

YOUR TESTIMONY

Tomorrow I promise to stop pretending about . . .

What's in the past is in the past.
I shouldn't ask about my boyfriend's
past relationships, right?

---

rule 51

Know something about your mate's past relationships.

*Y*ou've heard it said a hundred times, "People who don't know their history are doomed to repeat it." This doesn't simply apply to civil, world, or family history. The statement is probably most accurate when dealing with relationship histories. To learn about your boyfriend's past relationships without prying, spying, or breaking any laws can be an asset to you. You should be able to learn where his other relationships went wrong, and how you can avoid similar pitfalls. You may uncover pet peeves, girl issues, and other useful information. In any case, it should be a history class that you don't mind taking.

MY TESTIMONY

In any relationship I've ever had, I've always asked about past relationships. In a noninvasive way, I've learned how guys have been dumped, how they've elected to end relationships, and what situations make them uncomfortable. I'll ask, "How did your previous relationship end?" or "What was the most difficult obstacle in your last relationship?" I don't dwell on anyone's past, but I do utilize that past to understand how they may react in our relationship. I've always believed that a person who is secretive about past relationships cannot necessarily be trusted. But the hardest part about asking those kinds of questions was being ready to hear the answers and being asked the same questions as well.

BLUEPRINT

Knowing my partner's relationship history will educate me about some of the challenges that he has faced.

YOUR TESTIMONY

Make notes here about how you would begin a conversation with your boyfriend about his past.

Am I ever going to get over
my ex-boyfriend?

---

rule 52

You can survive heartbreak.

*M*illions have had their hearts broken and yet have gone on to find the "real" love of their lives. Survivors of abusive, destructive relationships have moved on to have loving, powerful, committed partnerships. Expect no less from yourself. Depression and loneliness may convince you that you will not find happiness again. But they are both liars. Time is yours, and happiness is just down the street and around the corner. Get walking!

MY TESTIMONY

My painful breakup with Bryce was a situation that I never thought I'd get over. As a twenty-year-old, I believed that I had a solid relationship with a decent guy. We both had big dreams, and determination flowed through our veins like blood. But after I sensed his commitment to me slipping and finally found out about his infidelities, we parted ways.

I wasn't thrilled about it, but it was absolutely necessary. I mourned that relationship for months. But hey, the rainbow comes after the rain.

BLUEPRINT

A relationship may have been part of my life, but it is not all of my life. My destiny awaits.

YOUR TESTIMONY

My heart was broken when . . .

What does compromise mean?

_____

rule 53

Be willing to resolve differences and work together in a relationship.

*E*verybody wants a relationship, but few people want to really work at it. Relationships are a meeting of the minds, where two people come together to share feelings, goals, and experiences. But in any relationship there's going to be disagreements, differences of opinion, and silly things. Sometimes you may get your way during an argument; other times you won't. Lasting relationships are give-and-take, up and down, and a lot of hard work. Enduring relationships don't break up at the first sign of trouble.

MY TESTIMONY

I like chick flicks—the emotional, tissue-consuming movies that make you laugh and cry at the same time. But who-ever I've dated has always liked shoot-'em-up, blood-and-gore movies. If we weren't willing to take turns in who selected the movies, I would have been going to the movies with my girls all the time or going by myself. Both of those options would have been fine, but neither would have done anything to build any of my relationships. Whenever I think about the times that I've watched the guts leaking out of larger-than-life figures onscreen instead of watching a hopeless, dying girl reach her goals, I know that I tried to make a relationship work.

BLUEPRINT

If I desire a lasting relationship, I must be willing to work hard and compromise when necessary.

YOUR TESTIMONY

The hardest part about compromising in the relationship is . . .

I'm somewhat curious about my boyfriend's crew. Should I try to get to know his friends?

―――――――

rule 54

Get to know his friends.

*J*f you ever want to know what a person is really like, get to know his friends. Friends showcase what a person's tastes are, what he favors, and what he's against. Who you choose to associate with speaks volumes about your character. After a game, or at the mall, basic conversations are the first step toward getting to know your mate's friends.

MY TESTIMONY

Max's friends were either athletes or hustlers. During the school year he hung with the ballplayers. In the summer, he hung with the dealers. I never fully understood how he could be friends with such different types of people. In his senior year of high school, when the football season was over, he began to hang out with more and more pushers. He even included a few drug users in his crew. By the end of that year, Max had lost faith that he'd get a college football scholarship, so he became an addict instead. I finally understood why he selected his particular group of friends. His friends represented what he believed he would become on his best days, and also on his worst.

BLUEPRINT

Getting to know my mate's friends will help me to learn about him.

YOUR TESTIMONY

I think my boyfriend's friends are . . .

At my school, it seems like most of the guys have two girlfriends. Is sharing your boyfriend with another girl normal?

---

rule 55

Boyfriend sharing is not mandatory.

It's on every soap opera, and many other television shows: scenarios where grown women are sharing husbands, fiancés, and boyfriends. It seems impossible to have a relationship that is exclusive. If you plan your life around television, it will be chaotic, hectic, and out of control. But it is absolutely possible to have a boyfriend that you're not sharing with your neighbor. It all depends on the type of guy that you have and the kind of relationship that you're working with.

MY TESTIMONY

A guy in a sociology class once told me that girls are supposed to share men. He ranted, "Polygamy is a worldwide accepted practice for a reason." The sharing of husbands is alive and well in many countries, but in the United States, guys who want to practice polygamy need to move to Utah. In that same class, a girl said, "Guys can't be faithful. So we're all sharing men anyway." I don't believe all guys are unfaithful. The girl who believes that definitely doesn't have a faithful guy.

BLUEPRINT

I can have a good one-on-one relationship if that is my desire.

YOUR TESTIMONY

I think girls who share boyfriends . . .

My parents don't like my boyfriend. Can I get them to like him?

---

rule 56

Some parents won't like anyone.

*M*any parents have said, "Nobody will ever be good enough for my daughter." Is that because the daughter is so great, or is it because everybody else is so horrible? Neither situation is usually true. More than likely it's because the parent is unwilling to accept that his child has found someone worthy to have a relationship with. A parent who always wanted the best for his offspring cannot believe that there is someone out there in the universe that can possibly equal his child. Is that thought ridiculous? Absolutely. Is the opinion harmful? Definitely. Is there much we can do about it? Not likely. I think most parents would love for their children to find good people to date. But parents have a lot more experience in life and can sometimes see things that their children can't. This includes the fact that parents can see a bad apple walking through the door when we think he's Prince Charming.

MY TESTIMONY

In some regard, I wanted my parents to like whoever I was dating. I wanted them to think that whoever he was, he was decent. But the fact is, every guy that I dated *wasn't* decent. Some of them were no good. Some of them weren't going to amount to anything, and my parents knew it already. Some of the guys were going to drain my energy and potentially damage my self-confidence. My parents weren't mean or preachy to anyone I dated, nor did they ever let me forget that I was more important to them than anyone that I was dating.

BLUEPRINT

My parents' experiences affect their feelings about the people I date.

YOUR TESTIMONY

I want my mom to like my boyfriend because . . .

*I've been getting a funny feeling
around my boyfriend lately.
He's never where he says he's going to be.
When I ask him certain questions,
he refuses to answer me.
What should I do?*

---

rule 57

When you keep feeling that your mate is lying, he probably is.

*Y*ou're probably not a psychic. But often when you're speaking to your boyfriend about where he spends his time, where he's going, or who he's been with, the hairs stand up on the back of your neck. A voice in your head says, "He's lying." But you silence the voice and pretend that you're believing his conversation wholeheartedly. Still, you know deep down that he couldn't spell "truth" if you gave him the first four letters.

MY TESTIMONY

Will was always used to having people obey his every wish. As a star athlete he received preferential treatment, he had a flock of groupies, and every basketball fan in the state knew exactly who he was. It wasn't funny then, but the truth didn't know who he was. He lied constantly to get whatever he wanted. And when he didn't feel like lying, he simply refused to answer questions. When I first met him, I couldn't sense the deceit in his character. Like so many other girls my age, I was caught up with his superstar aura. But behind the glow was an inwardly insecure person and an obnoxious guy. When we finally stopped talking, it was a relief, because my brain had grown tired of trying to separate lies from truth.

BLUEPRINT

I do not have to be in relationships with liars.

YOUR TESTIMONY

I got a funny feeling when . . .

*Am I destined to go through high school
never having a boyfriend?*

---

rule 58

Not everybody has a
high school sweetheart.

The reference to high school sweethearts is legendary. In television shows, movies, and magazines there appears to be an overall assumption that everyone who has ever attended high school had a high school sweetheart. Allegedly, everybody had that special somebody that they dated in high school, perhaps the first person that they said "I love you" to outside of their families. But as reality would have it, not everyone has or had a high school sweetheart. Many people may have gone out on a date in high school, but like thousands of miners, they did not strike gold. And that's okay. Your ability to have good relationships in the future is not based on whether or not you had a high school sweetheart.

MY TESTIMONY

Out of all the dates that I endured and all the boyfriends that I had, not one person sticks out in my mind as my high school sweetheart. Sure, some of the experiences were memorable, and some of them I'll actually still recall five years from now. But the imprint that they've left on my mind is fading fast. The fact is, high school dates become relatively insignificant once you begin college, and even less important when you begin your journey into full-fledged womanhood.

BLUEPRINT

A high school sweetheart is not a mandatory requirement in my life.

YOUR TESTIMONY

Ask some adults about their high school sweethearts. What they have to say may surprise you.

I tell my boyfriend one thing, and he does the opposite. What's happening?

---

rule 59

Know what your partner wants from you and the relationship.

Some boys want a girl to showcase in the mall. Others want somebody who they can talk to on the phone, and some want girls only for sexual reasons. Whatever your boyfriend wants, you need to know, so that you can decide if you're going to go along for the ride.

MY TESTIMONY

After a heated argument about how much time Bobby was spending with his frat brothers, I realized that he didn't know what I wanted from him. I would ask when we were going to the movies. He would promise that he'd take me, and then the next day he would give me the keys to his car so I could drive to the mall by myself. I'd suggest that we have dinner together on Saturday before we went hanging with our respective crews. He'd stop by Saturday afternoon with one of the frat brothers in tow and ask what was for dinner. He really didn't understand that I wanted our relationship to be about us spending time with each other. Bobby missed the whole point.

BLUEPRINT

It's in my best interest to communicate with my partner about our relationship.

YOUR TESTIMONY

It was hard for me to talk to _____ about . . .

My boyfriend's mother acts like she's
trying to get in between us.
Should I confront her?

---

rule 60

Some parents and families will get involved in your personal relationships.

Some parents are uncomfortable with their teens making life-altering decisions. Many parents are cool with teen dating, but then there are parents who want to pick who you go out with and where you go. They want to decide where and how you spend your money as well as what color your prom dress should be. If your parents aren't like this, your boyfriend's parents might be. It's hard to be someone's sole provider, protector, and nurturer for fifteen years and then, on the sixteenth birthday, to let go and say, "Bye-bye." Give the parents a break. Try to be understanding—even when it hurts.

MY TESTIMONY

Londell's mother never liked me. Whenever I'd visit him, she'd always be curt and excuse herself from the living room. Whenever I wasn't around, he told me stories of how she thought I believed that I was better than him. I guess she couldn't conceive that a girl from the suburbs could have a genuine liking for a guy from the projects. We always talked about our parents. He argued with his mom a lot about her feelings for me, but her opinions didn't disrupt our relationship. I accepted that she would always be his mom, and it wasn't necessary for her to like me.

BLUEPRINT

Most parents are trying to look out for their kids. I will accept that, even though I may not agree with their interference.

YOUR TESTIMONY

When _____'s mom said or did _____, I felt . . .

My boyfriend complains that
I'm too jealous. Can't he see that
I just care about him and
am protective of our relationship?

---

rule 61

Jealousy can destroy a relationship.

*J*ealousy is called the green-eyed monster for a reason. It can quickly become scary, unattractive, and out of control. It's crazy to think that once your boyfriend hooks up with you, he'll never speak to another girl. And even crazier to think that every girl on the planet who may walk past him or glance at him wants him. Yeah, you may not like it when he talks to other girls, but sometimes it's gonna be necessary, and it definitely isn't the end of the world. Be secure in who you are and your relationship, and you won't get as steamed when other girls talk to your man.

MY TESTIMONY

Denise had a crush on Bobby. Her open affection for him circulated around the campus like the college newspapers.

When we started dating, even I had heard about Denise's crush, and I wanted him to look me in the face and tell me what was going on. In that year, both Bobby and Denise pledged. During pledge week I remember her handing him something in line as I walked by. Every time I saw Denise, I got irritated. The thought that they would share the same pledge year infuriated me. I was jealous of her trying to create a bond when he had a girlfriend. And even though jealousy didn't totally destroy our relationship, it definitely shook the foundation.

BLUEPRINT

I will be secure in myself and not allow jealousies to destroy my relationship.

YOUR TESTIMONY

I felt jealous when . . .

*My boyfriend and I don't go
out together in public very much.
He tells me he's really private.
Should I be concerned?*

---

rule **62**

If your relationship is a secret, you should know why.

*N*o one knows that he's your boyfriend. He insists that you keep a low profile at school. Although he may have jewelry that you could wear to show the world, he won't let you wear it. Every time you bring up letting people know that you're an item, he dismisses the subject. What do you do? Some guys like their privacy because they don't want everybody to know about their relationships. Some guys are hiding more than one relationship, so discretion is a big deal. If you think your relationship is too much of a secret, ask him some direct questions. If he still refuses and doesn't give you a convincing explanation, dump him.

MY TESTIMONY

The universe was the only thing bigger than Will's ego. A star athlete who was favored by teachers, principals, journalists, and sports fans, Will thought he could have a girlfriend at every school, and no one would be the wiser. When I found out about another girl, he would say, "That's an old relationship. They don't know what they're talking about." But people did know what they were talking about, and they understood why Will and I never went anywhere in public. He was concerned about his other five girlfriends finding out. What a loser.

BLUEPRINT

If my relationship is a secret, I'm entitled to find out why.

YOUR TESTIMONY

I felt my relationship was a secret when . . .

My boyfriend is really jealous.

Doesn't that show that he really likes me?

---

rule 63

Jealous boyfriends can be dangerous.

"If I can't have you, no one will." It sounds cute at first. But when a guy really would rather end your life than allow you to move on, it's not funny at all. Jealous boyfriends, ones that don't want a girl to speak to another guy, sit next to one in the library, or converse with another dude in the mall, can be dangerous. Their simple love-themed statements can become threats, and eventually violent actions. Never underestimate how far one will go if his jealous urges take over.

MY TESTIMONY

When I decided to move into my own apartment my senior year in college, I don't think I realized how expensive everything was gonna be. When I went to Chicago to visit Bryce, I told him of the dinette set and the television that I wanted for my apartment. He didn't seem particularly interested in my apartment, and I mentioned that I was gonna talk to Will about it. Bryce immediately pulled the car over to said, "You can talk to him. Now get out of the car." In the middle of a bad area in Chicago, I was not getting out of the car. Somebody would have had to throw me out. Bryce was jealous of Will because Will was already a professional athlete, and he knew he couldn't compare to him on that level. When he started the car back up again, he drove me to my vehicle, and I didn't talk to him for a week.

BLUEPRINT

If I sense that a boyfriend is allowing jealousy to get the best of him, I must remove myself from that situation.

YOUR TESTIMONY

I noticed _____ was a jealous boyfriend when . . .

Is it okay to date someone
of another race?

_____

rule 64

Matters of race can impact a relationship.

*T*wo people who are really into each other rarely think about how their relationship affects other people. But race can bring out attitudes that we thought didn't exist. If friends or family don't want you to date someone of a different race, hurtful things may be said. Some opinions may make you question being in an interracial relationship at all. People will reminisce about experiences that they had seventy-five years ago to illustrate a point. In America, we suffer from the worst cases of racism, but still the world is not as it was in the 1850s. If you are moved to date someone who does not look like you, be moved by your heart, spirit, and soul.

MY TESTIMONY

When I was in high school, interracial dating was very limited. The few people who did date outside of their race were outcasts and considered "weird." In one situation, I recall a girl named Bridget who was 100 percent African-American but dated only white guys. She wore a weave attached to the back of her head and had the personality of Foxy Brown on a bad day. One day she was leaning against the wall, crying hysterically. I never really socialized with her, but all the noise caused me to go over to her and ask how she was doing. She could barely lift her head up to speak. I found out that in a recent heated exchange her 100 percent Caucasian boyfriend created a scene, broke up with her, and called her a nigger, all at the same time. Bridget was devastated and so humiliated that all she could do was stand in the hallway and cry. As I reflect on this experience, I don't know what hurt Bridget more, realizing that her boyfriend didn't love her or that her so-called color-blind boyfriend called her a nigger in front of a crowd of people. Whatever the case may be, Bridget got over it and continued to date Caucasians.

BLUEPRINT

Other people's opinions on race will not affect my attitude toward interracial relationships.

YOUR TESTIMONY

I think interracial dating is . . .

*Is it a bad idea to ask
my brother for advice on boys?
I don't necessarily want him
so involved in my business.*

---

rule 65

The best male advice comes from your brother, cousin, or uncle.

*M*ost girls go to other girls for advice concerning boys. But some of the best advice concerning guys will come from other guys. A man that cares about you unconditionally like a brother, cousin, or uncle can be objective enough to put himself in your position, yet he'll still see any situation from a male point of view. When you're wondering how a guy would feel or react in certain instances, ask a real guy.

MY TESTIMONY

My overwhelming love for Bryce had me doing a Stevie Wonder impression during the summer of my junior year in college. Bryce was such a great storyteller that a five-minute conversation with him would have me believing that Nike would start giving away Jordans every day of the week. During that summer, I told my brother of all the wonderful things that Bryce was doing. I even talked about what we were going to be doing together. For the month of June, my brother listened to my stories without judgment, but by August, Ricky had had his fill of the Paul Bunyanesque tales that Bryce was telling me. After I told my brother another story about why Bryce wouldn't be coming to visit me, he looked at me in an odd way and said, "Everybody has to get their man." The look in his eye told me that I had to wake up, grow up, and realize that Bryce was as phony as the Rolex watches on New York Avenue in Washington, D.C. I appreciated my brother for being real with me when no one else would.

BLUEPRINT

I will utilize the knowledge of my male relatives when seeking advice regarding guys.

YOUR TESTIMONY

Which male relatives can you go to for advice? Make a list.

*My girls are complaining that
I never want to spend time with them
since I started a new relationship.
I feel that I have to choose my girls
or my boyfriend.*

---

rule **66**

Just because you have a boyfriend doesn't mean you can't spend time with your girls.

*B*oyfriends come and go, but friendships with your girls can last your entire lifetime. It's great to have and go out with a boyfriend, but it's also great to talk to your girls and share in your experiences. Gaining a boyfriend doesn't mean that you have to get rid of your girls. Every relationship in your life serves a purpose. Girlfriends will always fulfill needs that a boyfriend cannot. When you alienate your girlfriends just because you've picked up a mate, you risk being alone in the event that your relationship with this particular guy doesn't last forever.

MY TESTIMONY

Jade used to kick the girls to the curb every time she had a boyfriend. She wouldn't call us anymore, didn't want to listen to our problems, and spending time with us was not even a possibility. If she found a guy, it was all about him, and the girlfriends lost a member of the crew. Later in life, Jade finally realized that every time you gain a boyfriend, you don't lose your girlfriends. As a result, all of her relationships are better.

BLUEPRINT

I will cherish my relationships with my girls even when I have a boyfriend.

YOUR TESTIMONY

I'm making an extra effort to spend time with my girls by . . .

Why does breaking up have
to be so bitter?

---

rule **67**

Some relationships will end badly.

$\mathcal{N}$o one is perfect. People have terrible tempers, and some folks resist change. In a relationship that seemed to be happy all the time, breaking up can bring acrimonious monsterlike qualities out of a partner. The guy who used to be kind and loving is now mean and hateful. You can try to be as friendly as possible, put extra sugar in the Kool-Aid, but the guy only wants you and the relationship to continue. He's not interested in being friends; he doesn't care about your feelings. Oh, well, you got to move on.

MY TESTIMONY

After being in a relationship with a guy who was too busy to spend any time with me, too self-centered to treat me well, and too despicable to care, I realized that the union could only end on bad terms. For the entire partnership, I had been sensitive to the demands of his athletic commitments, his enormous ego, and his never-ending immature behavior and girl-crazy ways. I was both halves of the relationship. I was the person crying and the shoulder that was cried on. For all of my efforts, I was emotionally discarded and physically mistreated. This relationship left me with scars that took thirteen years to heal. When the relationship dissolved, it did so on bad terms. I called him a few bad names, wished he'd never been born, and then I moved on with my life.

BLUEPRINT

It's not always possible to create a happy ending to a bad relationship.

YOUR TESTIMONY

This relationship ended badly because. . . .

*My boyfriend has a lot
of problems at home.
What should I do with all his drama?*

---

rule 68

Be supportive to a partner who is experiencing problems at home.

*I*t seems that some people always have something going on. If it doesn't involve school, it involves family, work, or friends. A lot of problems that people have are within their control, but unfortunately a slew of other challenges are completely out of their hands. Boyfriends who are having problems at home feel weak, vulnerable, and unloved. Strive to be understanding and thoughtful to your partner, especially when things are bad on the home front. After all, you would want similar support if the shoe was on the other foot.

MY TESTIMONY

My friend Todd's mother was an alcoholic. Mrs. Johnson would get nasty and abusive to her son when she was drunk. She said things like, "I wish you weren't my son," and "You'll never amount to anything." Every time the alcohol took control of her mind, Todd had to leave the house to avoid insults and being struck. When I received his calls from the pay phone, I knew that his mother had been drinking. As a teenager, I really didn't know anything about Alcoholics Anonymous. All I could do was listen and pray that his mother would find a way out of the bottle.

BLUEPRINT

I will be compassionate to my mate, especially during times of emotional upheaval.

YOUR TESTIMONY

Think about some of the situations that your friends have gone through recently.

I felt sorry when . . .

Should I give my ex-boyfriend
a second chance?

---

rule 69

Most old boyfriends don't deserve a second chance.

Time will play tricks on your memory. It will cause people to rethink their decisions and actions. Old boyfriends can look even better after some time has passed. The effects of time will make deep wounds seem shallow and make major transgressions seem like minor infractions. Many guys woo their old girlfriends into believing that they have improved. An old flame may approach you, and his story seems fresh. He may not resemble his old trifling self. Your heart wants to give him a chance, but your head is saying no. Most old boyfriends don't deserve a second look. The ship has left the dock, and they weren't on it. When you were with them, they didn't appreciate you, so why bother? Trust the decisions from your past; they've helped you to get where you are today.

MY TESTIMONY

For the most part, I don't believe in second chances in relationships. I think you have one time to get it right, so you better work hard. But in one case I did reestablish a relationship after an amicable breakup. And again, the union didn't work. The same personality clashes reappeared, and the unnecessary criticisms that he was always wielding were as unwelcome as they were before. Looking back, I know I reopened the relationship because I was bored, not because I believed anything between me and Gary had changed. The brief reunion wasted time and energy for both of us.

BLUEPRINT

I will focus on my future and not my past.

YOUR TESTIMONY

If one of my ex-boyfriends asked for a second chance, I would say . . .

Can a girl and a guy just be friends?

---

rule 70

Guys and girls can have platonic relationships.

*a*s rare as it may be, girls can have solid friendships with guys and vice versa without the slightest intent of a relationship. Friendships born out of common interest allow for this. For example, a guy and girl who both play basketball can talk about their skills, games, and so forth and work with each other to become better. These kinds of friendships are based on truth and honesty and don't involve deception or an angle.

MY TESTIMONY

One of my best friends in high school was a guy. He didn't date girls, but he was still one of my best friends. When I was attending high school, young people were not coming out of the closet like they are today. If they did, Horatio would have probably admitted his homosexuality. Regardless of his sexual orientation, we still talked about life, careers, and dating. I dominated most of the dating conversations. Later in my life and as an adult, I still have three best friends who are guys. As a matter of fact, they are all heterosexuals. We don't talk about relationships as much as we talk about guiding our careers, the entertainment business, and just life's daily hustle. My friendships with the guys in my life help me to see a male perspective in a lot of my business enterprises. It takes special people to have friendships with members of the opposite sex when there is so often an underlying attraction.

BLUEPRINT

I can have a platonic relationship with a guy who shares my interests.

YOUR TESTIMONY

My platonic relationship with _____ is strong because . . .

My boyfriend never takes me out, saying he can't afford to. But he's always buying things. Should I think something is up?

---

rule 71

A boyfriend who never takes you anywhere is definitely sending a message.

*J*f you really like someone, then you're gonna want to spend time with that person and do things for that person, whether it's going to the movies or watching a football game. People who care about you want to do things with you. Guys who complain of not having any money to go on dates find money when the new basketball shoes hit Foot Locker. Excuses are often given when somebody doesn't want to spend time with you but doesn't want to tell you. If you are getting excuses instead of quality time, you should probably find someone else to be in a relationship with. Guys who want to be a part of the fun must be more industrious at being a part of the funding.

MY TESTIMONY

Shauna's boyfriend always told her that he wanted her to spend time with him. She was constantly telling the girls how much he loved her and all the nice things he wanted to do for her. He wrote her romantic poems and love letters, but when it came time for them to go out or spend time together, he always had an excuse. He continually told her about having to study and having other commitments. After hearing so much talk about her boyfriend and what he was "supposed" to be doing, I finally told Shauna that it wasn't real for a guy to claim to be all lovey-dovey in letters and on campus, and then when it came to spending time together, he couldn't make it a priority. After several more weeks of broken promises and no time served, Shauna finally dumped him.

BLUEPRINT

I will not remain in a relationship where I cannot spend quality time with my partner.

YOUR TESTIMONY

Make a list of some of the things that you and your boyfriend do together. Compare this list to the things that you would like to do.

There's a secret I haven't told anyone:
I like girls. Am I just going through
a weird phase?

---

rule 72

Lesbianism is not a fad.

*H*igh school teachers, guidance counselors, and teen youth advocates have talked about the increase in teen girls who claim to be lesbians. It has been described in many urban centers as "the new thing." In Philadelphia many teen lesbians are calling themselves "DTO"—an acronym that means "Dykes Taking Over." Choosing to be a lesbian is not like picking the new lip gloss of the day. Historically, lesbians nationwide have been ridiculed, hazed, beaten, and even lost their lives because of their sexuality. It's not cool to pretend or play with a person's feelings on this level, because too many people get hurt.

MY TESTIMONY

In a recent visit to Philadelphia while promoting my book *The Blueprint for My Girls*, I was speaking with a group about the issues that are affecting African-American girls. We discussed issues of self-esteem and self-love, and a teen in the audience said, "What about the girls in my school who wrote 'Dykes Taking Over (D.T.O.)' on the walls in the bathroom?" This teen went on to say that teen lesbians are intimidating, bullying, and sexually assaulting "straight" girls in their pursuit of "Taking Over the School." Obviously violent tactics aren't the way to express your sexual orientation. In my research with teen girls, I'm learning that many "straight" girls aren't going to the bathroom in their public schools because they don't want to be cornered and felt up by their lesbian classmates. The teen lesbians that I've spoken to have given me mixed responses. Some of the girls believe that they have always liked girls, while some of them have dated boys and recently found dating girls to be more satisfying. An older lesbian I spoke with was insulted by the number of teen girls who claim to be lesbians because it's apparently "the in-thing in their school." Choosing to be a lesbian is not like picking out a pair of shoes. If it's that simple for you, you're not thinking hard enough.

BLUEPRINT

Even if it appears that lesbians have become more popular, that does not mean that liking girls is for me.

YOUR TESTIMONY

I think girls liking other girls is . . .

Sure, sometimes my boyfriend seems a little quirky, and sometimes he acts strangely. But there's nothing to worry about, right?

---

rule 73

A mentally unbalanced person brings chaos to the relationship.

*M*any of us have met people that we believed were crazy. Jokingly, we shrugged off bizarre behavior and searched for the normalcy in those individuals. But there is a point of being too crazy—a point where psychosis is no laughing matter. Getting involved with a person who has shown crazed behavior can be a serious mistake. People whose mental capacities are not fully functional are gonna be a headache to deal with, to say the least. Life is too short to have a relationship with someone you already know is crazy.

MY TESTIMONY

From the outside, Paul looked normal. He spoke intelligible English, enjoyed sports, and cared about his personal appearance. He was excellent at playing board games and really laughed when I tried to tell jokes. One day my friends and I were going to the bowling alley, and he didn't have a way to get there. About an hour after we arrived, Paul showed up to hang with us. When I asked him how he got here, he explained that he had taken his father's car. Sirens went off in my head. As I was telling him how stupid it was to take a car without permission, he was trying to explain that he really wanted to see me. All I could think about was: What if I needed money for a prom dress—would this fool rob a bank?

BLUEPRINT

I will not downplay a person's mental deficiencies. My life is much more important than that.

YOUR TESTIMONY

Jot down a few things that struck you as odd that another person did.

I'm attracted to a guy out of state.
What my boyfriend doesn't know
can't hurt him, right?

———

rule 74

There are costs associated with two-timing your boyfriend.

*a*nyone can be in one relationship and then find themselves attracted to someone else. But what are you going to do about the attraction? Is your current relationship worth more to you than your curiosity? Many make the mistake of believing that they can have two boyfriends at once. They think, "One's in school with me, and the other's across town. Nobody will ever know." But amazingly, someone always finds out. When you decide to two-time one boyfriend, realize that you're two-timing both. And you could lose both relationships when they find out. In the unlikely event that you can manage two boyfriends without anyone knowing, you will always know the truth. You know about your lying, betrayal, and insincerity. How would you feel if your boyfriend was doing this to you?

MY TESTIMONY

During the summer of my junior year in college, Dalvin, an eccentric, nosy, trouble-making friend of Bryce waged a bet. He felt that every girl who his friends were currently dating had cheated on them, so he was going to begin an all-out search to discover who cheated, when, and with whom. When Bryce told me, I almost passed out. I had one small skeleton in my closet. He asked, "If you cheated on me, you might as well tell me now, and I won't be mad. 'Cause if Dalvin finds out something, it's over." Well, three months prior to this bet, I had been asked out by a guy while I was still dating Bryce. Bryce wasn't acting right at the time, so I went out on the date. Nothing happened, and I never called the guy again. At the talk of Dalvin exposing everybody's girlfriend, I was definitely feeling the heat. Was I gonna admit that I almost cheated on Bryce, even though it would break up our relationship? I don't think so. I waited for Dalvin to call my bluff, and he never did. But he could have.

BLUEPRINT

If I decide to two-time my boyfriend, I will be willing to lose him if I'm exposed.

YOUR TESTIMONY

What are your thoughts on two-timing? Could you ever do it? What would you do if it happened to you?

Why should I listen to what somebody else
is saying about my boyfriend?
That person is probably just jealous.

---

rule 75

Listen to both sides of the story.

*E*ven in bad situations, there are two sides to every story. Whenever an altercation occurs, we think that we know the full scope of the situation. But nothing is as it seems, so we must have the facts, obtain additional information, or do the research. Jumping to conclusions prevents us from reaching the truth or giving anyone the opportunity to explain. And it leaves us yearning to really know what happened. No matter how bad the story seems, you should find out about it from both sides.

MY TESTIMONY

When I decided to tell a good friend that her boyfriend had been cheating on her with her best friend, I didn't think that she would listen to me. But she did. I told her boyfriend, Brian, that I was gonna tell her, and he called her and admitted his indiscretion. When my friend confronted the girl about having sex with Brian, she refused to tell the truth. She refused to admit it, even when Brian admitted that he had done it. Because they were never close, it was easy for her to say I was lying to destroy them or that I didn't like the girl, so I must be lying. And even though my friend knew that the girl was lying, she listened to her side of the story. After it was all over, my friend was glad that she had heard what everybody had to say. On that day, she learned who was really looking out for her.

BLUEPRINT

I will not assume that I know the facts of any situation. I will seek out both sides of the story.

YOUR TESTIMONY

I had to listen to both sides of the story when . . .

People are always saying that you should be friends with someone before dating them. But isn't love supposed to be an immediate feeling?

---

rule 76

Friendship is the basis of every relationship.

True friendship is underrated, and yet it is the foundation of practically every relationship that we have. The best love relationships survive because of a genuine liking and respect for each other. Friends protect, care for, and appreciate one another despite differences of opinion, social background, or superficial things like hair color. Friendship, in its essence, can withstand the test of time. It all depends on the individuals. Don't ever think that you can be the best significant other to someone if you can't be a good friend to anyone.

MY TESTIMONY

When I first met Marcus, I noticed how attractive he was from the start. He wasn't hard for me to look at, and he was very easy to communicate with. Instead of immediately dating, after our first meeting, we talked about life, work, and family. We got to know each other on a platonic level before our first date. When we had lunch on our first date, I remember thinking, "If I never have a relationship with this guy, I've at least made a new friend." And to this day, we still have the best friendship.

BLUEPRINT

I will be an excellent friend.

YOUR TESTIMONY

My friendship with _____ is good because . . .

My ex-boyfriend has a new girlfriend.
Every time I see them together,
I feel sick to my stomach.

---

rule 77

It hurts when your boyfriend has another girl.

*E*ven the most self-confident, positive, and upbeat individual can feel a twinge of envy when they see an ex-boyfriend with his new girlfriend. It's human nature to think, "I should still be his girlfriend," "She doesn't look better than me," or "They're both wack." But just as easily as these thoughts enter your mind, they should exit. Dwelling on the new couple will only make you miserable. Remember you have other concerns, like who you're going to the movies with on Friday.

MY TESTIMONY

I make it a practice not to know what my ex-boyfriends are doing. What difference does it make to me? When Dan and

I were getting to know each other, the school year was coming to a close. I didn't feel comfortable starting a relationship when we were going to be apart, so we agreed to keep in touch over the summer. Whenever we talked, it inspired me to write great poetry, and there was a wonderful connectedness to our conversations. When we got back to school, our relationship moved into full swing, and for a couple of months, I really believed that this would be the guy that I would marry. When he graduated and moved, we still kept in touch. Thoughts of us having a permanent relationship were always in the back of my mind. Then one day he told me that while we were apart, he had sexual relations with a girl, and now she was having his baby. He told me that they had only been out a couple of times, and yet they'd been out enough for them to be expecting a child. Talk about hurt. Not only had Dan hurt me by sleeping with some one-date chick, the one-date chick was having his child. That was the beginning of the end of that relationship.

BLUEPRINT

Although I may feel hurt in seeing an ex-boyfriend with a girlfriend, I will not allow the pain to be my focus.

YOUR TESTIMONY

List some instances when you were hurt by an old boyfriend.

I feel as though I've outgrown my boyfriend, but my sense of commitment keeps me in the relationship.

---

rule 78

If your personalities don't click, don't push it.

There is a saying that goes, "Don't try to put a square peg in a round hole." In other words, if some things don't belong together, don't force them. The same philosophy should be applied to relationships. Trying to be in a relationship with someone you can hardly have a conversation with isn't a good idea. Just because you think he's cute doesn't mean he's the right fit for you.

MY TESTIMONY

If I said that I wanted to go the movies, Gary wanted to go to the beach. If I felt like wearing shorts on a particular day, Gary commented that I should have worn a sundress. The ways that we differed were unbelievable. We always had fun talking or hanging out, but we had to overcome 100 percent differences of opinion before the fun started. As much as I liked Gary and enjoyed his company, I had to face the fact that this guy was not the one for me.

BLUEPRINT

There is someone out there for me, so I don't have to force any relationship.

YOUR TESTIMONY

What are some good qualities that you've liked about a certain person, and what are the qualities that you disliked?

My boyfriend does some irritating things that get on my nerves. I've told him about them, but he still keeps doing them.

---

rule 79

You can't change anyone but yourself.

So many girls want to change their boyfriends for the better. Maybe a boyfriend doesn't always go to class on time. Maybe he doesn't apply himself when completing his homework. Whatever his malady, it's in the female DNA to want to improve our male counterparts. Most guys will pretend that they want change, and some will even go along with your suggestions. But the fact is, change is often a difficult process that requires enormous commitment. Wanting someone to change doesn't mean that they will. In the end, we only have the power to alter our own being.

MY TESTIMONY

I didn't want my friend Shawn to drop out of high school. I couldn't stand knowing that he was on the corner getting high every night into the wee hours of the morning. I hated knowing that the same fingers that gripped a baseball bat were burned at the tips from holding a cocaine-laced marijuana joint. But there was no conversation that we could have, no lecture creative enough, to stop Shawn from going down the road of destruction. When our relationship ended, he looked at me, his eyes saying, "I'm going places that I won't allow you to visit." I couldn't comprehend the pain in his eyes. Today, I'm just thankful that he cared enough not to take me with him.

BLUEPRINT

I will not attempt to force change onto anyone or be frustrated when my suggestions for change are not implemented.

YOUR TESTIMONY

Name some people that you've wanted to change, and why.

It's six months since I broke up with my boyfriend, and I'm still crying myself to sleep every night.

---

rule 80

Depression is not an option.

*I*f your relationship breaks up, I personally give you permission to be sad for a day, maybe two. I'll allot you one box of tissues. And you can call your best friend and talk all day for the two days about him, but that's it. You mustn't sink yourself into a perpetual state of sadness over a boyfriend who's moving on with his life. This must not happen. Clinical depression has become widespread over the years. Suicides have been committed because depression has taken over mind, body, and soul. Even if it doesn't seem like it, you have your entire life ahead of you. You can be sad for two days, only two, and then let the good times roll.

MY TESTIMONY

I was chilling at Bryce's house while he went out to run

some errands. While straightening up, I noticed a huge Valentine's card addressed to him that was not sent by me. I grabbed my stomach, overwhelmed by pain. The room was spinning, and I had to sit down, but I didn't feel comfortable with where I was or who I was. It was June, so that meant he'd been cheating on me for at least five months. I felt like a complete fool. When he came back to his house, he told me some more lies about the girl, how she liked him and he didn't like her. But I knew that he was lying. For the next couple of days, I listened to sad love songs and sat in my room. I wouldn't call Bryce or take his phone calls. I relieved my pain, anguish, and embarrassment through the music that soothed my soul. I used up three-quarters of a box of tissues, and then I decided our relationship was over. Forever.

BLUEPRINT

I will not become overly depressed when relationships end. Everything happens for a reason, so it's probably a good thing.

YOUR TESTIMONY

It has been hard getting over . . .

PHASE 3

Intimacy

After you get to know someone and make a commitment, becoming physically intimate is often the next step. It is important to remember that even sex that people consider casual exposes their innermost being. The body is a temple, and once you've allowed others to enter, your body and mind are different from that point forward. You should not expect allowing someone to know you intimately to leave you with no feeling at all.

Is everyone having sex,
and am I the only one missing out?

———————

rule 81

Everybody isn't having sex.

*M*any magazines and television shows want you to think that every teen is sexually active. A lot of the music we hear on the radio has such sexually suggestive lyrics that we feel there is nothing more important in life. But life is more than sex. And media images are misleading at best. The overall teenage pregnancy rate has gone down in the last fifteen years, and it isn't because more teens are having sex.

MY TESTIMONY

As a sophomore in college, I lived in a dorm room. The dormitory experience allowed everybody to really get to know each other. When me and some of the other girls weren't doing anything on a Friday night, we'd sit in each other's rooms, paint our nails, and talk. During one of those evenings, I found out that some girls who were nineteen years of age still had not had sex. It was mind-blowing, but such a relief. In high school, there was always the thought that everybody was having sex. Obviously that wasn't the case, as many people made it to college without having any sexual experiences at all.

BLUEPRINT

Whatever I hear about people having sex isn't necessarily true, and it doesn't affect what I'm going to do with my body.

YOUR TESTIMONY

A lot of people are talking about sex because . . .

I performed oral sex on my boyfriend.
Oral sex isn't as serious
as "real" sex, right?

---

rule 82

Oral sex is sex.

*a*ccording to *Webster's*, sex is defined as the joining of a male and female sexual organ. That means oral sex—when a sexual organ is touched by a person's mouth—has to be some form of a sexual act. A person cannot get pregnant by receiving or performing oral sex, but because of the presence of bodily fluids, sexually transmitted diseases, herpes, and HIV can all be contracted through oral sex. People like to say that oral sex is safer sex, but it's only safe as it relates to pregnancy.

MY TESTIMONY

When I was in graduate school, the majority of my classmates were white. I spent many hours socializing with them and talking about our shared as well as different experiences. One night we were discussing oral sex practices as they currently existed in black and white communities. A classmate said that among her groups of friends, oral sex was mostly had prior to actual sexual intercourse, and that her girlfriends were mostly givers of oral sex and not receivers. As I recall, the classmate said that oral sex was something her friends performed on guys that they liked but didn't necessarily have to be in a relationship with. I told her that in the black community, oral sex wasn't even considered if that person was not your serious boyfriend, and the thought of performing oral sex prior to having sex was completely out of the question for my circle of friends. For the classmate and her crew, oral sex could be utilized as a get-to-know-you measure; for my mostly African-American crew, oral sex was not ever a possibility if you were not in a serious, serious relationship. But now, as I talk to teen girls, I know that times have changed, and it doesn't seem that oral sex is as restricted a behavior as it once was.

BLUEPRINT

I will consider my decision to participate in oral sex as seriously as if it was typical sexual activity.

YOUR TESTIMONY

My opinion on oral sex is . . .

Abstinence is hard.

How long should I wait?

---

rule 83

Abstain from sex as long as possible.

$\mathcal{I}$f having sex is a game of dominoes, the act itself knocks down the first game piece, which then knocks down the safe-sex domino, which hits the "Did the condom break?" domino, which hits the HIV domino while at the same time hitting the "Is my period late?" domino. Having sex starts a series of reactions that most teens aren't ready for, and most are simply afraid of. Sex is a serious decision, and unlike dominoes, it's not a game.

MY TESTIMONY

I've tried to live my life without any regrets. The mistakes I've made, I've mostly learned from. But my first sexual experience was pointless, painful, and definitely could have been saved for a much later date. How does a fourteen-year-old who is just learning to deal with her own individuality handle decisions like birth control, condom usage, and the like? How does a fourteen-year-old deal with feeling sexually mistreated and raped? These were the questions that I had to ask myself. I often felt inadequate and sad because I was involved in sexual situations that I could hardly understand. Instead of being able to focus on growing as a stress-free fourteen-year-old with the world at my fingertips, I was burdened by sex and the problems associated with it.

BLUEPRINT

Whether to have sex is a decision that I will not take lightly.

YOUR TESTIMONY

I think girls are or aren't ready to have sex because . . .

What does
a gynecologist do?

---

rule 84

Gynecologists are here to help us.

*M*any people have physician-related phobias—folks just don't want to go to the doctor. Some of us don't want to know what's wrong with us because we believe that it would hurt physically to find out. But once you become sexually active, a trip to the gynecologist is mandatory. The gynecologist makes sure there are no vaginal infections, bleeding irregularities, or reproductive issues. Undetected female problems can become worse when we don't visit the doctor.

MY TESTIMONY

My first trip to the gynecologist at fifteen years of age was pretty scary. I didn't know how to relax while an internal examination was being done, so it was painful. But it was short. I learned over the years to make blowing breaths when having my annual examination so it doesn't hurt as much. It still doesn't feel like I'm being tickled, but I can get through it without hollering.

BLUEPRINT

My gynecological health is important to me. I will go to the doctor for my routine checkups as well as when something goes wrong.

YOUR TESTIMONY

My first gynecologist visit was . . .

I believe that sex is a natural part of life. What harm will come to me if I have sex with whomever I choose?

---

rule 85

Be highly selective when considering with whom to have sexual relations.

Young women are liberated today in ways we could have only dreamed about seventy-five years ago. According to magazines, TV, movies, and radio, women can sleep with whomever they desire and not worry about being labeled. The media would have you believe that you can entertain as many sexual partners as possible, and as long as you wear a condom, you're not in any real danger. Unfortunately, the media often delivers a distorted view of reality. Yes, it's true that women are freer now to have sex with various partners, but in some circles you will still be labeled "whore," "slut," and the like. These labels are hurtful and can damage a healthy self-image. And although condoms reduce the spread of STDs and HIV, they're only 80 percent effective against pregnancy. Needless to say, condoms do break, leaking bodily fluids. So if and when you make that decision to have sex, think about it. You could end up being attached to that partner for the rest of your life.

MY TESTIMONY

During their first few weeks on campus freshmen are often referred to as "fresh meat." It's a term that connotes the vulnerability of new students attending college. When I was attending college, older male students would literally camp themselves outside the freshman dorms with their branded arms and fraternity colors, trying to bait the newest girls on the block. Unbeknown to us freshmen, these upperclassmen already had serious girlfriends. All they were trying to do to us was have sex and go through as many freshmen as they could until their girlfriends returned to campus. Not every girl got caught in this trap, thank goodness. But I felt for the ones that did, because I know they were probably looking for more from the guy than sex.

BLUEPRINT

Sex is not a come-one, come-all proposition.

YOUR TESTIMONY

When I think about selecting sexual partners, I think . . .

What kinds of birth control exist?

rule 86

Be informed of your birth control options.

$\mathcal{W}$hen we don't know about something, it can seem scary and make us feel uncomfortable. A lack of knowledge of birth control options can cause us to make mistakes that could have been avoided. There is a lot of information about birth control pills, patches, and diaphragms in the marketplace. There is no reason that we shouldn't know it.

MY TESTIMONY

My cousin has been a health educator working with youth organizations for many years. She talks to teens about their sexual health. In many of her cases, she has worked with girls who've become pregnant and don't know how it occurred. In some instances, girls have become pregnant without knowing about the simplest birth control methods, like condoms and/or birth control pills. People who are having sex should know how to prevent pregnancies if having a child isn't their goal.

BLUEPRINT

Knowing about birth control is necessary if I am thinking about or engaging in sexual activity.

YOUR TESTIMONY

I know about many different birth control options. For example, if I wanted to try some birth control methods, I would . . .

Can you get pregnant if you're only making out?

rule 87

You can get pregnant without having sex.

*P*regnancy occurs when sperm fertilizes the egg. If two people are lying together naked, and a man's penis leaks sperm near the opening of the vagina, the sperm can travel and fertilize the egg. The girl could definitely become pregnant. Many pregnancies have occurred in this manner. Do not believe that the vagina has to be penetrated in order for your egg to be fertilized.

MY TESTIMONY

Guys who are taking you on the road toward a sexual destination may say, "We don't have to do it, let's just lay here together." You may think, "As long as his penis doesn't enter my vagina, then I'm okay." A nurse who visited my high school social studies class told us of many instances where young women have become pregnant this way. I couldn't believe it. As I looked around, most of my classmates were shocked by this information. I've never had that experience, nor has it happened in my circle of friends, but just knowing that it could happen changed our attitudes, perceptions, and behavior about "not having sex."

BLUEPRINT

I will not believe myths about pregnancy.

YOUR TESTIMONY

Pregnancy could affect my life by . . .

*What are stars thinking when
they see young, pretty girls backstage?*

---

rule 88

Going backstage or to the hotel room of a star is serious business.

*R*ap stars, professional athletes, and entertainers are of-fered sex with no strings attached in every city that they visit. Groupies are lined up at the entrances to back-stage and overflowing from the lobbies of hotels. Most au-tograph seekers are not seven-year-old kids who shove autograph books into stars' hands. They're usually girls or young women seeking to spend the night. Any girl who puts herself backstage or in the lobby of a rap star, an ath-lete, or an entertainer should know that he isn't expecting to have a long, drawn-out get-to-know-you conversation. Wake up and grow up. Being backstage is about sex, and it is not a dress rehearsal.

MY TESTIMONY

As a journalist, I've been at the hotels where superstars are staying, and the number of sexually available women is mind-boggling. Dressed in see-thru attire, G-strings, and platform heels, women go into hotel rooms, shower stalls, and tour buses to pleasure the star as well as the star's entourage. Some of these women follow stars and athletes city to city in hopes that they can have sex. Easy, commitment-free consensual sex is expected when girls visit hotel rooms and backstage. I've overheard women being told to perform certain acts, and if they didn't, they were escorted out of the room and their friends were brought in to take their places. It happens in every city, in every hotel, after the concert or the basketball game.

BLUEPRINT

Backstage is a place for groupies and sexmongers.

YOUR TESTIMONY

If I ever got the opportunity to go backstage, I . . .

My boyfriend tells me that a condom isn't necessary because we're both faithful to each other.

---

rule 89

No sex without condoms, period.

*M*any guys have said, "Sex isn't enjoyable wearing a condom," "I can't climax wearing a condom," or "I can't fit a condom." Those statements are lies meant to trick you into having sex without the use of a condom. If your partner refuses to be safe, you should refuse to participate. The risks of venereal disease, HIV, and pregnancy are not worth a few minutes of pleasure.

MY TESTIMONY

In a college health class, we talked about condoms. Most of the guys said that condoms were uncomfortable or that condoms took away from the sexual experience. Most of the girls said that they felt sex with condoms felt the same as sex without. But when the question was raised about who should suggest using a condom between two people, the class got quiet. Is it okay for girls to carry condoms? A lot of guys in my class didn't think so. They argued that a girl who carries condoms is looking to have sex all the time and therefore is some kind of whore. That opinion couldn't be further from the truth. A girl who carries a condom believes that she should protect herself even when her partner refuses to do so.

BLUEPRINT

Sex without a condom is not for me.

YOUR TESTIMONY

Guys who say that they won't wear condoms . . .

*Old guys are always making passes
at me. What is their problem? Do they
think they seriously have a chance?*

---

rule 90

The existence of dirty old men is not your fault.

It has happened in so many families, and yet child molestation remains a dirty secret. Common-law husbands, uncles, and fathers have forced their daughters and nieces to have sex with them. Even grandfathers have been found sexually assaulting their offspring. Young girls have been threatened and beaten to keep quiet while they've been raped by men they are supposed to trust. The rape victims go on with their lives—confused, angry, and blaming themselves for the treacherous acts that were committed against them. "If only I wasn't home then. If only I hadn't sat on the couch. If only Mom didn't have to work . . ." But it is not young girls' fault that predators live among them. We must report child molesters to the proper authorities, rid ourselves of shame, and save ourselves.

MY TESTIMONY

At a book signing in Baltimore, a woman approached me and shared her recent experience of finding out that her common-law husband was sexually molesting her daughter. My heart ached as she detailed how her daughter's behavior had become angry and violent. The woman explained that her daughter's tragedy was tearing her family apart. She tried to talk to her daughter, but her daughter didn't want to communicate. The mother has gone to law enforcement authorities and apparently been given the runaround. If her daughter reads this book, I want her to know that she did nothing wrong. She was not acting improperly to be at home, watching TV or doing her homework. The actions of the child molester were wrong, criminal, and totally inappropriate. I truly believe that he will be punished for his actions.

BLUEPRINT

If I'm ever put in a situation where I've been taken advantage of by a dirty old man, I will not internalize those feelings. I will report his actions to the police.

YOUR TESTIMONY

I've met dirty old men. They've acted or said . . .

I'm sixteen, and my boyfriend is nineteen.
Is it really against the law for us
to have sex, even when we both agree?

---

rule 91

Having sex with older guys can be against the law.

Statutory rape occurs when an adult—a person eighteen or older—has sex with a minor. A minor is usually defined as a person under the age of eighteen. States have mandated statutory rape laws to protect young women from being the target of manipulative, oversexed males. Many men use their physical and financial well-being in addition to emotional savvy to encourage girls to have sex with them. Whether or not a young woman gives consent is irrelevant. It does not matter if the parties are "boyfriend and girlfriend." Statutory rape laws are set up to protect us for a reason.

MY TESTIMONY

Having a sugar daddy seems so 1970s. But older men, aka

sugar daddies, are often prowling high school parking lots looking for potential girlfriends. In my circle of friends, the story of Rochelle and Tahib was common knowledge. Rochelle was extremely poor and lived in the inner city. When she got to high school, she hooked up with a hustler named Tahib, who was about fifteen years older than her. She became a diva overnight. He bought her all the nicest clothes, jewelry, and furs. Whatever she saw on TV or magazines, she had hanging in her closet. Everybody knew that Tahib was breaking the law every time he had sex with Rochelle, but nobody said anything—not even Rochelle's mother. Since Tahib was never reported for having sex with a minor, their relationship could have gone on forever. Without passing judgment, it seemed okay for Rochelle to date an older man as long as he was providing for her and her family financially. However, when he was eventually arrested, prosecuted, and imprisoned for selling and distributing narcotics, Rochelle was left out in the cold. She realized that dating an older man wasn't everything she thought it would be.

BLUEPRINT

Statutory rape laws are set up to protect me from older men.

YOUR TESTIMONY

If an older guy wanted to date me, I would . . .

My chemistry teacher is young,
and I enjoy flirting with him.
Is that wrong?

––––––––––

rule 92

Teachers should not have flirtatious, sexual relationships with their students.

*M*ost teachers are great people. But every now and then, among the phenomenal teachers and coaches, the system allows a predator into the midst of the children. Schools in every state have fired and/or suspended personnel for inappropriate acts involving minors. School employees are commissioned to teach, nurture, assist, and guide the students. Confusing, sexually violating, and preying upon the innocence of young girls is not supposed to be in their job description. Report to the police and your parents any teacher that you feel is behaving in an unprofessional or sexual way toward you.

MY TESTIMONY

At the college level, most students are eighteen years of age and older and thereby legally able to make decisions about their sexual partners. Although some colleges institute policies forbidding the professors from having relationships with students, at my graduate school at least one of our professors had a couple of relationships with undergraduate students. Though it wasn't against the law, the feeling of some of the faculty and the students was that of discomfort. No one really said, "The professor dating the student was wrong," but it was clear that the girls he dated were viewed as different from the rest of the student body. In fact his dates were ostracized, and many people questioned the professor's judgment. Because there are millions of people on the planet, I believe that teachers and professors can find sexual partners without looking in the classroom.

BLUEPRINT

I will report any teacher's inappropriate behavior.

YOUR TESTIMONY

I have a teacher that I think is cute and . . .

Is there really such a thing
as a date-rape drug?

---

rule 93

Watch your drink and food at all times.

$\mathcal{J}$t doesn't matter what you're drinking; if you're in a public place, a club, a gym, or wherever, keep your eyes on your cup. And never drink from it again if you've lost sight of it. This goes for your plate as well. If you leave it on the table, don't eat from it again. In the last five years much has been written about date-rape drugs. These are drugs that make a person incapable of protecting themselves or saying no. They can leave you powerless to fight off a rapist or attacker. If you feel that you have been given a date-rape drug or been raped and can't remember what happened the night before, go to the hospital. Your blood will need to be checked, and you'll need an examination. Predators who use date-rape drugs often prey in an area until they're caught. Only by reporting our experiences with the date-rape drug will we be able to diminish its use.

MY TESTIMONY

There have been numerous reports of girls being tricked into taking the date-rape drug. Instances have occurred at campus parties and in clubs, when someone has given a girl a drink and then shortly thereafter, the girl passes out. Newspapers across the country have interviewed young women who have awakened in unfamiliar places and whose clothes have been soiled. In many cases the last thing that the girl remembers is being given something to drink by somebody that she thought she could trust.

BLUEPRINT

I will keep a watchful eye on everything that I eat or drink in public places.

YOUR TESTIMONY

I've heard about the date-rape drug . . .

If I have a baby,
I'll become a more motivated person.
It'll force me to be more responsible.

———————

rule 9 4

Being a single parent isn't always a motivator.

*J*n the past ten years, myths about single parenthood have arisen. People have begun to say that being a single parent can motivate you because now you have someone else to look out for. Now, you're going to be more responsible. For some single parents, raising children has heightened their awareness and assisted them in focusing on their life goals. For other parents, single parenthood has been a weight that they blame for not achieving their dreams and robbing them of their youth. Who you are on the inside can be improved or worsened when you become a single parent. However, you don't have to find which side you're on by becoming a parent prematurely.

MY TESTIMONY

In one of my girls' workshops, which took place at a church, we were discussing teens becoming parents. Out of a class of about twenty, a sixteen-year-old girl was already a parent, and another fifteen-year-old was seven months along. The sixteen-year-old said, "I can hardly do any of the things I used to do. Everything involves taking care of my daughter. I remember when I used to take a nap after school. I can't even do that now." Another girl who was in the workshop said, "I have friends who have kids and they say, 'I gotta finish school and get a good job for my kid.'" When I was in high school, the teen pregnancy rate was much higher than it is today, and there was a greater stigma associated with being a teen parent. The girls who had children did not socialize or have the fun that we had. They were busy babysitting. If having a child can motivate you to become a better person, then that better person lives within you anyway, and you don't have to give birth to find that out.

BLUEPRINT

Parenthood is a huge responsibility and a decision that I should make when I am ready to devote my time to raising a child.

YOUR TESTIMONY

I think becoming a parent when you're in your teens is . . . I know teen mothers who . . .

I'm already pregnant.

Should I just go ahead and marry the guy?

rule 95

Don't have a baby, move in with someone, or get married before *you* want to.

any girls exiting high school and college are propositioned by their respective boyfriends to have a child, move in together, or get married. The guys often want somebody or something that they can hold on to. For whatever reason, many young men encourage their girlfriends to have babies when they have no real intention of raising the children with them. Moving in together can cramp personal space, especially if you really don't want to see that person every day. Younger married couples are getting divorced less than five years after getting hitched. Anyone under twenty-four years of age shouldn't feel pressure to have a child, move in, or get married. Your entire life is ahead of you. If your boyfriend threatens to leave you if you don't do either, dump him first.

MY TESTIMONY

On the eve of my senior year in college, I had a conversation with Bryce about having kids. He told me, "If you want to have a kid, it's your decision." As we continued our discussion, it seemed that he was encouraging me to have a child, although I had not finished college. I had a bunch of other goals to accomplish. After that conversation, I knew that I wasn't ready to have children, and I knew that if Bryce thought it was solely my decision, he'd probably leave all the responsibility of having a child and raising it to me. What would my goals have amounted to then?

BLUEPRINT

I will not be pressured into having children or getting married.

YOUR TESTIMONY

I will be ready to have children or get married when . . .

*My boyfriend suggested that I have
sex with his friend, since he and
his boy share everything.
Have you ever heard of such a thing?*

---

rule 96

Sex with his friend is a bad idea.

Guys who hardly speak can be creatively verbose when talking girls into doing hurtful things. Scenarios where girls are having sex with their boyfriend's crew have been played out on television and in film. In most recent cases, the situations don't end well. The girls are being objectified. They are called whores after the experience, and their self-esteem sinks to brand new lows. Even in cases where the girls seemed to enjoy being passed around, they never receive what they desire—love, respect, and commitment. No girl should believe that having sex with her boyfriend's crew is going to make their relationship stronger.

MY TESTIMONY

When I hear rap songs refer to girls being passed along through their crews, I shake my head. The girls that they are talking about are groupies and prostitutes. They are not talking about their main girl having sex with their friends. I attended an entertainment conference several years ago where approximately seven prostitutes had sex with about thirty-five DJs and music industry executives in the span of six hours. Some of these guys were married, and some had girlfriends. In college there were stories about fraternity parties where a girl might have had sex with a bunch of guys in the fraternity. But this girl was not thought of highly, wasn't respected, and quite frankly was the campus joke.

BLUEPRINT

I will not associate with any guy who asks me or expects me to have sex with his friends.

YOUR TESTIMONY

If a guy ever asked me to have sex with his friends, I would . . .

Should I be tested for HIV?

---

rule 97

If you've been engaging in high-risk behavior, you should get tested for HIV.

*a*lot of people would rather be ignorant of their HIV status, figuring, "If I don't know, I can't get depressed about it." But what they mean is, "If I don't know, I don't have to be responsible about infecting anyone else." In the past fifteen years, medical breakthroughs have extended the life expectancy of people living with HIV. AIDS is no longer the death sentence it once was. Consequently, the people who refuse to get tested for HIV are also saying, "If I don't know my HIV status, I won't be able to save my life."

MY TESTIMONY

When I was first tested for HIV, it was part of some additional blood work that I was getting during a routine gynecological visit. It was during the early nineties, when people with AIDS were dying at an epidemic rate. As the lab technician drew my blood, I couldn't help but think how my life would change if I found out that I was HIV-positive. I would have to think about the people that I dated. I would have to tell my parents, and they would be preparing my burial before their own. These thoughts ran through my mind and made me sad. That was nearly fourteen years ago, long before the drugs came on the market that have been lengthening the lives of people with HIV and AIDS. Today, I don't think people should be as afraid of being tested for HIV as they were back then. Equip yourself with knowledge, get tested, and know your status.

BLUEPRINT

Getting tested and treated for HIV could save my life and the lives of others.

YOUR TESTIMONY

I'm not afraid to be tested for HIV because . . .
I would get tested if . . .

I think my ex-boyfriend gave me herpes.
Should I confront him about it?

---

rule 98

Confront the person who you believe infected you.

There aren't many conversations more difficult than telling someone that you've contracted a venereal disease. If you've had sex only with that person prior to contracting the disease, then you must be confident in raising the issue. For example, "I didn't have this venereal disease before I had sex with you." Most guys will deny giving you a disease, but truth will always be on your side. Venereal diseases do not float through the air. The only way to get them is by someone infecting you. The only way to get cured is to seek medical help and confront the germ-spreader so that he'll get help as well.

MY TESTIMONY

"Happy one day, devastated the next." That's the best description of a college classmate who after an annual pelvic examination found out that she had an STD. She only had one boyfriend with whom she was sexually active. After a call from the doctor, she told her boyfriend of the doctor's results. He accused her of cheating on him, broke up with her, and left her wondering if she could get gonorrhea from a toilet seat. Well, of course she couldn't. But before he'd admit that he had cheated and infected her, he'd rather lie, violate her trust, and break her heart.

BLUEPRINT

People who spread venereal diseases need to be confronted.

YOUR TESTIMONY

In my school rumors circulated about venereal diseases. The talk was . . .

I'm pregnant, and I know I don't have the
resources to properly raise a child.
But abortions are wrong, right?

---

rule **99**

Abortion is a tough decision to make.

Terminating a pregnancy can be an awkward, heart-wrenching experience. You don't want to hurt any-one, but you don't want to carry a child full-term at this stage of your life. Thousands of women have made the de-cision either to have an abortion or to bring a baby into the world. The key to your decisions will be your love of self, your relationship with God, and your closest counsel.

MY TESTIMONY

I'm not an advocate of abortion. On this issue, I definitely believe we should avoid becoming pregnant with children that we don't plan. But I've been there as a young person—in a relationship that was going nowhere, when I didn't feel like I could count on anyone. I've been there with the thought of having to take care of a baby and knowing that an unplanned pregnancy could change the course of my life forever. I had to make a tough decision, and maybe it wasn't the right decision. But I thought about it, and I prayed on it. And I realized that since I was facing this circumstance, I was here for a reason.

BLUEPRINT

I will be responsible for my body so that I won't have to make decisions involving abortion.

YOUR TESTIMONY

I think abortion is . . .

Afterword

When it comes to dating and relationships, there's a lot of information floating around. Every month, magazines feature articles and dating quizzes with titles such as "Is He Your Guy?" "Do You Know if Your Partner Is Being Faithful?" and the like. And we all have friends who are eager to weigh in on our dating, relationship, and love experiences.

Good advice is great, but unfortunately all advice isn't good. This book was put together to offer great advice for the times when there is no one you feel you can talk to, or when you've listened to someone who gave you bad advice. *The Blueprint for My Girls in Love* was inspired by situations that have actually happened to me, my friends, and my family. As the saying goes, there is nothing new under the sun. I'm hoping that there will be a testimony in here that can help you with your decision making.

Some people may disagree with some of the rules I've included in the book. But I believe that these rules will guide you to have better dating, relationship, and love experiences. People say that you can't read life in a book, that you must go out and live it. That's absolutely true. However, there's nothing wrong with going out into life armed with some knowledge. *The Blueprint for My Girls in Love* presents that kind of information.

I have also included lists of people and organizations that can help you navigate life. You need more than my testimonies; you need real phone numbers and real people in your time of need. I have personally worked with many of the organizations listed in these appendices. One of the biggest mistakes that I made as a teen was not asking for help when I faced a crisis. Please don't make that mistake. You have more resources in this book than I had in my entire high school and college career combined. Use this to your advantage.

I've said it before, but it's worth repeating: sex complicates things. People who are bent on having sex with you will say anything to prevent you from realizing that sex is their only true goal. You've probably seen women on talk shows describe how men became less attentive or focused after the women went to bed with them. Don't let anyone tell you that sex doesn't powerfully change the dynamic of any relationship. It absolutely does. When you get to a point in your life when you believe that you're ready to become intimate with someone, reread the rules in *The Blueprint for My Girls in Love* that pertain to sex. These rules are here to assist you in making the best decision that you can.

Your life is fully ahead of you. Please don't underestimate your value as a person, or how much you are loved by your family. Remember that personal relationships can get out of hand, so we all must be careful in whom we talk to and deal with. As you go out into the dating world, you must remember to protect yourself—emotionally, physically, and sexually.

Be happy, be safe, be encouraged.

Who Can I Talk to About Dating, Relationships, and Intimacy?

There is a network of people in your life who can assist you when you're facing your most difficult challenges. I have listed them below.

MOM

Some people can talk to their mothers about everything. A lot of folks can't talk to their mothers about anything. When I was younger, I didn't feel comfortable talking to my mom about the various dating and relationship crises I was facing. I believed that she would judge me and I didn't want her to remind me that I wasn't as smart as I thought I was because of mistakes I had made. So I suffered through experiences that she would have helped me through if I had only opened up to her. Some moms will judge you and treat you differently after you ask for help. Others won't, because, believe it or not, they've been there. Try as much as you can to have open communications with your mother. There are lots of things that you are going through that she has experienced as well.

REAL AND PLAY BIG SISTERS AND COUSINS

I didn't have a "real" big sister to talk to, but I connected with my older brother's female friends, who were often two to three years older than me. When I had questions about dating, relationships, or sex, they were more than willing to tell me the real deal. They could tell me which guys were dogs, which ones already had girlfriends, and who was seen kissing whom. "Big sisters" gave me a glimpse into the dating game before I was even allowed to date. You can find "big sisters" in various activities that you participate in like basketball, volleyball, and the like. Meeting older girls through being tutored is also a great way to meet a "big sister."

You might also find a "big sister" in one of your older cousins. You can never underestimate the family factor. Some of my cousins are ten years older than I am, yet we are very close. When I was fifteen, they were twenty-five and very mature. Yet at the same time, they weren't as old as my mom. I could talk to them, and I knew they could give me advice, but they wouldn't tell on me or judge me for asking questions.

I recall having a conversation with one of my cousins about abortion. She wasn't exactly pro-choice, but in our discussion I learned about why she chose to have a child at a time in her life when many others thought it was inconvenient. And I also got the sense that if I needed her to support a pro-choice decision, she would have been there for me.

RESPECTED TEACHERS

There were a couple of teachers in my high school that I absolutely connected with. I didn't necessarily have a class with them, but they oozed an aura that said, "I understand where you've been, and I know where you're trying to go." I respected how they spoke to other students, how they carried themselves, and even how they dressed.

My geometry teacher and I connected right off. She had

taught my brother years before, and she was a strong black woman—somebody that I admired. She would often ask me, "Yasmin, how are *you* doing today?" She emphasized *you* because she wanted me to know that she wasn't simply asking if I understood my geometry homework. I didn't immediately start divulging my innermost thoughts with her, but I was glad she asked. One day I was totally distracted in class. I had received threatening phone calls the night before from a fellow female student. As I left her classroom that day, my teacher called out to me and said, "Yasmin, are you okay? You don't seem like yourself." I just shook my head. Ten minutes later I was fighting in front of the cafeteria. Maybe had I shared what was on my mind, the fight would have never happened.

The teachers with whom you feel a kinship can assist you through crises. They will try to do whatever they can to help you.

AUNTS

My aunts and I never lived in the same city (or the same state, for that matter). But whenever I talk to them, I can share various experiences from my life. Talking to an aunt about a bad situation is like talking to your mom without the guilt. A good aunt knows that when she helps you out, she's indirectly helping her sister or brother.

SCHOOL GUIDANCE COUNSELORS

Today's guidance counselors are equipped to deal with sexual abuse, rape, and crisis intervention issues. Guidance counselors are there to help you out of painful, dangerous, and volatile situations. Monday through Friday, it is the guidance counselor's job to be there for you. Of all the people I've met in any school system, the guidance counselors are the least judgmental, and particularly proactive when it comes to seeking resolutions to a student's problems. Additionally, if they believe that you are in harm's way, they can assist you to safety. You don't have to feel that you're all alone.

CRISIS HOTLINES

There are crisis hotlines all over the United States. These are toll-free numbers set up to help people who are having problems. When I was in college, I volunteered to answer calls for the local battered women's hotline. The women I spoke with were usually married with children and scared to death. Most of the women who called weren't experiencing battery for the first time. When I spoke with these women, I told them how courageous it was for them to call. The next section lists Web sites and 800 numbers of organizations that are set up to assist teenagers in crisis. You are anonymous to these call centers, and they are there to give you information. Call them!

CHURCH FOLK

Churches, like society, are full of all sorts of people. Some folk show up on Sunday to see who is wearing what, some are there to be a part of the church family, and countless others are there for reasons beyond my grasp. However, since my first book, I've been working with churches across the country, and I have met wonderful people in every one. Most every church includes people of great faith who will not allow a young person to remain in a painful situation, no matter how many people have to be shamed. They will reach out to assist you because they believe it is their calling. Church folk like that will not always carry an official designation like youth director, deaconess, or pastor's wife; you will know who they are by the way they treat and interact with others when they think no one is around. You can tell who they are by their warmth, their attitude, and their actions.

What Organizations Can Help Me?

I selected the following organizations because I've interacted with each while promoting my first book. Although many of these programs emphasize empowerment and community service, they also understand that young people go through personal problems and will discuss those topics. Develop relationships with other girls and the staff at these organizations. It's worth your time.

NATIONAL

The mission of BIG BROTHERS AND BIG SISTERS is "to help children reach their potential through professionally supported, one to one relationships." They serve young people ages 6 through 18. This agency provides excellent mentorship and role model opportunities.
www.bbbsa.org
(215) 567-7000

THE BOYS AND GIRLS CLUBS OF AMERICA has clubs throughout the United States. "Club programs and services promote and enhance the development of boys and girls by instilling a sense of competence, usefulness, belonging and influence."
www.bgca.org
(404) 487-5700

EMPOWERED CHILDREN's vision is to empower, educate, equip, enlighten, and elevate children ages 7–17, providing them with the necessary tools to understand their identity, purpose, and destiny.
www.empoweredchildren.com
(800) 377-1302

GIRL SCOUTS OF THE USA are "dedicated to helping girls everywhere build character and gain skills for success in the real world." Girl Scout chapters throughout the United States are an excellent place for dialogue and peer discussions.
www.girlscouts.org
(800) GSU-SA4U

GIRLS INC. has innovative programs to help girls confront subtle societal messages about their value and potential, and prepare them to lead successful, independent, and fulfilling lives." Girls Inc. chapters throughout the United States often work with schools via the after-school program. Lifelong friendships are started in places like these, and there are plenty of trustworthy administrators to connect with.
www.girlsinc.org
(800) 374-4475

The NATIONAL CENTER FOR VICTIMS OF CRIME is the nation's leading resource and advocacy organization for crime victims. The mission of the center is to forge a national commitment to help victims of crime rebuild their lives.
www.ncvc.org
(800) FYI-CALL

The mission of PLANNED PARENTHOOD is "to provide comprehensive reproductive and complementary health care services in settings which preserve and protect the essential privacy and rights of each individual."
www.plannedparenthood.org
(800) 230-PLAN

RAPE, ABUSE, AND INCEST NATIONAL NETWORK NATIONAL SEXUAL ASSAULT HOTLINE is the number to call if you are a victim or know someone who is a victim of rape, abuse, or incest.
(800) 656-HOPE

Teens are twice as likely as other age groups to be victims of violent crime. The National Center for Victims of Crime's TEEN VICTIM PROJECT "offers supportive counseling, practical information about crime and victimization, referrals to local community resources, as well as skilled advocacy in the criminal justice and social service systems."
www.ncvc.org/tvp
(800) FYL-CALL, or e-mail: gethelp@ncvc.org

TEENWIRE.COM is the leading Web site for teens needing information about sexual health. "It gives you the facts about *sex* so that you can use this information to make your own responsible choices."
www.teenwire.com

The URBAN LEADERSHIP INSTITUTE specializes in developing youth programs for communities and provides products for youth and youth groups based on leadership development, violence prevention, and self-awareness.
www.urbanyouth.org
(877) 339-4300

With various chapters and community-based programs, the YWCA "draws together members who strive to create opportunities for women's growth, leadership, and power in order to attain a common vision: peace, justice, freedom and dignity for all people."

www.ywca.org

(202) 467-0801

LOCAL

The BLOSSOM PROGRAM FOR GIRLS works with girls between the ages of 12 and 18, assisting with community-service opportunities, mentoring, workshops, and other activities. This program is run by the Youth Empowerment Mission of Brooklyn.

www.girlsblossom.org

(718) 857-2447

COOL GIRLS, INC., "dedicated to the self-empowerment of girls in low-income communities," serves girls living in Fulton and DeKalb Counties in Georgia.

www.thecoolgirls.org

(404) 420-4362

The IN THE LOOP PROGRAM is a fee-based program that provides rising high school juniors and seniors with support related to scholarships, postsecondary college options, career development, and conflict management. In addition, In the Loop also provides empowerment workshops and production opportunities for young people.

www.intheloopprogram.com

(404) 508-4612

SISTER MENTORS: "Our mentoring of girls of color includes sharing with girls some of the challenges women of color encounter in pursuing their education and strategies they devise to successfully move forward."
www.sistermentors.org
(202) 775-0946

The SLEDGE GROUP is based in Harlem, New York, and provides mentoring, tutorial services, and parent support to youth between the ages of 9 and 18. The program is dynamic in many ways, and its services are provided at no cost to participants.
www.sledgegroup.org
(718) 597-5099

YOUTH SERVICE PROJECT, INC. is a youth-development agency in Chicago that provides a lot of services, including substance abuse counseling, at-risk counseling, a girls mentoring program for Latina and African-American girls, job training, graphic design classes for youth and community members, a studio program where students can learn to mix their own music, and more.
www.youthserviceproject.org
(773) 772-6270

What Are the Different Kinds of Birth Control, and How Do They Work?

This information was provided by the Office on Women's Health in the Department of Health and Human Services.

There are many methods of birth control that a woman can use. Talk with your health-care provider to help you figure out what method is best for you. If you discover that you're not comfortable with a particular method, you can try another one.

Keep in mind that most birth control does NOT protect you from HIV or other sexually transmitted diseases (STDs) like gonorrhea, herpes, and chlamydia. Other than not having sex, the best protection against STDs and HIV is the male latex condom. The female condom may give some STD protection.

Don't forget that all of the methods described below only work if they are used correctly. Be sure you know the correct way to use them. Talk with your health-care provider, and don't feel embarrassed about talking with her or him again if you forget or don't understand.

Know that learning how to use some birth control methods can take time and practice. Sometimes health-care providers assume you already know how. For example, some people do not know that you can put on a male condom inside out, or that you need to leave a "reservoir" or space at the tip of the condom to collect the sperm when a man ejaculates.

The more you know about the correct way to use birth control, the more control you will have over deciding if and when you want to become pregnant.

Here are the available birth control methods, with estimates of effectiveness when used correctly.

CONTINUOUS ABSTINENCE. This language is consistent with the office on Women's Health. This means not having sexual intercourse at any time. It is the only sure way to prevent pregnancy. This method is 100 percent effective at preventing pregnancy and sexually transmitted diseases.

PERIODIC ABSTINENCE, OR FERTILITY AWARENESS METHODS. A woman who has a regular menstrual cycle has about nine or more fertile days, when she is able to get pregnant, each month. Periodic abstinence means you do not have sex on the days that you may be fertile. In order to practice this method, you need to keep a written record of when you get your period, what it is like (heavy or light blood flow), and how you feel (sore breasts, cramps). You should also check your cervical mucus and take your temperature each day with a basal body thermometer, and record these in a chart. This is how you learn to predict, or tell, which days you are fertile or "unsafe." You can ask your health-care provider for more information on how to record and understand this information. This method is 75 to 99 percent effective at preventing pregnancy.

CONDOM. Condoms are called barrier methods of birth control because they put up a block, or barrier, to prevent sperm from reaching the egg. Male condoms, which are put on an erect penis, come in many varieties and brands. Only latex or polyurethane condoms are proven to help protect against STDs, including HIV. "Natural" or "lambskin" condoms made from animal products also are available. Lambskin condoms are not recommended for STD prevention, however, because they have tiny pores that may allow for the passage of viruses like HIV, hepatitis B, and herpes. Condoms can only be used once. You can buy them at a drugstore. Condoms come lubricated (which can make sexual intercourse more comfortable and pleasurable) and nonlubricated (which can also be used for oral sex). It is best to use lubrication with nonlubricated condoms if you use them for vaginal or anal sex. You can use KY Jelly or water-based lubricants, which you can buy at a drugstore. Oil-based lubricants like massage oils, baby oil, lotions, or petroleum jelly will weaken the condom, causing it to tear or break. Always keep condoms in a cool, dry place. If you keep them in a hot place (like a billfold, wallet, or glove compartment), the latex breaks down, causing the condom to tear or break. Male condoms are 86 to 98 percent effective at preventing pregnancy. The female condom is worn by the woman. It is made of polyurethane, is packaged with a lubricant, and may protect against STDs, including HIV. It can be inserted up to eight hours prior to sexual intercourse. Female condoms are 79 to 95 percent effective at preventing pregnancy. There is only one kind of female condom, and its brand name is Reality. You can purchase it at a drugstore.

WITHDRAWAL. Withdrawal is not the most effective birth control method. It works much better when a male condom is used. Withdrawal refers to when a man takes his penis out of a woman's vagina (or "pulls out") before he ejaculates, or has an orgasm. This stops the sperm from going to the egg. "Pulling out" can be hard for a man to do, and it takes a lot of self-control. When you use withdrawal, you can also be at risk for getting pregnant *before* the man pulls out. When a man's penis first becomes erect, there can be fluid (called pre-ejaculate fluid) on the tip of the penis that has sperm in it. This sperm can get a woman pregnant. Withdrawal also does not protect you from STDs or HIV.

SPERMICIDES. You can purchase spermicides in drug

stores. They work by killing sperm and come in several forms—foam, gel, cream, film, suppository, or tablet. They are inserted or placed in the vagina no more than one hour before intercourse, and left in place at least six to eight hours after. You may protect yourself more effectively against getting pregnant if you use a spermicide with a male condom, diaphragm, or cervical cap. There are spermicidal products made specifically for use with the diaphragm and cervical cap. Check the package to make sure you are buying what you want. All spermicides have sperm-killing chemicals in them. Some spermicides also have an ingredient called *nonoxynol-9*, which can protect you from the STDs gonorrhea and chlamydia. Nonoxynol-9 will not protect you from HIV. Some women are sensitive to nonoxynol-9 and need to use spermicides without it. Spermicides alone are about 74 percent effective at preventing pregnancy.

ORAL CONTRACEPTIVES. Also called "the pill," these contain the hormones estrogen and progestin. A pill is taken daily to block the release of eggs from the ovaries. It also lightens the flow of your period and protects against pelvic inflammatory disease (PID), ovarian cancer, and endometrial cancer. It does not protect against STDs or HIV. The pill may add to your risk of heart disease, including high blood pressure, blood clots, and blockage of the arteries. If you have a history of blood clots or breast or endometrial cancer, your health-care provider may advise you not to take the pill. You will need a prescription and visits to your health care provider to make sure you are not having problems. The pill is 95 to 99.9 percent effective at preventing pregnancy if used correctly. Today's pills have lower doses of hormones than earlier birth control pills. This has greatly lowered the risk of side effects. However, there are both benefits and risks associated with taking birth control pills. Benefits include having more regular and lighter periods, fewer menstrual cramps, and a lower risk for ovarian and endometrial cancer and pelvic inflammatory disease (PID). Serious side effects include an increased chance, for some women, of developing heart disease and high blood pressure. Minor side effects include nausea, headaches, sore breasts, weight gain, irregular bleeding, and depression. Many of these side effects go away after taking the pill for a few months.

IUD (intrauterine device). There are various intrauterine devices. An IUD is a small device that is shaped in the form of a T. Your health-care provider places it inside the uterus. The arms of the Copper T IUD contain some copper, which prevents sperm from making their way up through the uterus into the fallopian tubes. If fertilization does occur, the IUD prevents the fertilized egg from implanting in the lining of the uterus. The Copper T IUD can stay in your uterus for up to ten years. The Progestasert IUD contains the hormone progesterone, the same hormone produced by a woman's ovaries during the monthly menstrual cycle. The progesterone causes the cervical mucus to thicken so sperm cannot reach the egg, and a fertilized egg cannot successfully implant into the lining of the uterus. The Progestasert IUD can stay in your uterus for one year. The *intrauterine system, or IUS (Mirena),* is a small T-shaped device like the IUD that is placed inside the uterus by a health care provider. It releases a small amount of a hormone each day to keep you from getting pregnant. The IUS stays in your uterus for up to five years. IUDs and IUSs do not protect against STDs or HIV. They require visits to your health-care provider for insertion, and to make sure you are not having any problems. Not all health-care providers will insert an IUD. IUDs and IUSs are 98 to 99 percent effective at preventing pregnancy.

DEPO-PROVERA. With this method women get injections, or shots, of the hormone progestin in the buttocks or arm every three months, administered by a health-care provider. Depo-Provera does not protect against STDs or HIV. It is 99.7 percent effective at preventing pregnancy.

DIAPHRAGM OR CERVICAL CAP. The diaphragm is shaped like a shallow latex cup. The cervical cap is a thimble-shaped latex cup. Both come in different sizes, and a health-care provider needs to fit you for them. Before sexual intercourse, you use these devices, along with spermicide (to block or kill sperm), placing them inside your vagina to cover your cervix (the opening to your womb). The diaphragm is 80 to 94 percent effective at preventing pregnancy. The cervical cap is 80 to 90 percent effective at preventing pregnancy for women who have not had a child.

THE BIRTH CONTROL PATCH (ORTHO EVRA). This is a skin patch worn on the lower abdomen, buttocks, or upper body. It releases the hormones progestin and estrogen into the bloodstream. You put on a new patch once a week for three weeks, then do not wear a patch during the fourth week so that you can have a menstrual period. The patch is 99 percent effective at preventing pregnancy, but it appears to be less effective in women who weigh more than 198 pounds. It does not protect against STDs or HIV. You will need to visit your health-care provider for a prescription.

THE HORMONAL VAGINAL CONTRACEPTIVE RING (NUVARING). The NuvaRing is a ring that releases the hormones progestin and estrogen. You place the ring up inside your vagina to go around your cervix (the opening to your womb). You wear the ring for three weeks, take it out for the week that you have your period, and then put in a new ring. The ring is 98 to 99 percent effective at preventing pregnancy. You will need to visit your health-care provider for a prescription.

EMERGENCY CONTRACEPTION. This is *not* a regular method of birth control and should never be used as one. Emergency contraception, or emergency birth control, is used to keep a woman from getting pregnant after she has had un-protected vaginal intercourse. "Unprotected" can mean that no method of birth control was used. It can also mean that a birth control method was used but did not work—like a condom breaking. Or a woman may have forgotten to take her birth control pills, or may have been forced to have sex when she did not want to. Emergency contraception consists of taking two doses of hormonal pills twelve hours apart, and started within three days after having unprotected sex. These are sometimes wrongly called the "morning-after pill." The pills are 75 to 89 percent effective at preventing pregnancy. Another type of emergency contraception is having the Copper T IUD put into your uterus within seven days of unprotected sex. This method is 99.9 percent effective at preventing pregnancy. Neither method of emergency contraception protects against STDs or HIV.

FOR MORE INFORMATION . . .

You can find out more about birth control methods by contacting the National Women's Health Information Center at (800) 994-WOMAN (9662), or the following organizations:

Food and Drug Administration
Phone: (888) 463-6332
www.fda.gov

Planned Parenthood Federation of America
Phone: (800) 230-7526
www.plannedparenthood.org/

Index

Abortion, 207–8, 212
Abstinence, from sex, 175–76, 222
Abuse, 71–72, 188–89, 217
Advice. *See* Resources
Age
  and dating, 11–12
  and sexual relations, 188–89, 191–92
AIDS, 203–4
Appearance, 37–38, 43–44, 49–50
Approaching people, 19–20
Arguments, 85–86, 113
Attention
  getting someone's, 19–20
  to surroundings, 65–66
Aunts, 213

Big Brothers, 215
Big Sisters, 215
Birth control, 175, 181–82, 222–27
Blossom Program for Girls, 218
Boyfriends
  criticism of you by, 107–8
  dislike of your friends by, 87–88

ex-, 39–41, 77–78, 111–12, 145–46, 161–62
ex-girlfriends of, 77–78, 109–10
expectations of, 125–26
of friends, 39–41, 83–84, 99–100, 157–58
friends of, 87–88, 115–16, 201–2
friends sleeping with, 157–58
male advice about, 137–38
as mentally unbalanced, 153–54
never having, 123–24
and parents, 119–20, 127–28
past relationships of, 109–10
physical abuse by, 71–72
and problems at home, 143–44
sex with friends of, 201–2
sharing, 117–18
stories about, 157–58
talking to friends about, 101–2
See also Ex-boyfriends; *specific topic*
Boys and Girls Clubs of America, 215

About the Author

YASMIN SHIRAZ is an empowerment speaker, entertainment journalist, author, and entrepreneur. A graduate of Hampton University and Morehead State University, Shiraz uses her sociology training to empower young people through her books, writings, and speaking engagements.

As an empowerment speaker, she includes among her topics the "Blueprint for My Girls" empowerment series, transitioning into womanhood, decision-making skills for young people, self-awareness is power, entrepreneurship, and her signature "How to Get into the Entertainment Business" tour. She has spoken at numerous colleges nationwide and has presented her work for sororities, social organizations, political organizations, and the like.

She is perhaps best known as a journalist who has interviewed such celebrities as Sean "P. Diddy" Combs, Jay-Z, Jada Pinkett-Smith, Nas, Queen Latifah, Johnnie Cochran, Lil' Kim, Martin Lawrence, Brandy, and others. For many years she owned the most successful urban entertainment magazine on college campuses, *Mad Rhythms*, which reached over four million students. In addition she has written articles for such respected publications as *Black Enterprise*, *Upscale*, *Impact*, and the *Electronic Urban Report*.

She has authored the nonfiction works *The Blueprint for My Girls: How to Build a Life Full of Courage, Determination & Self-Love* and *The Blueprint for My Girls in Love: 99 Rules for Dating,*

Relationships, and Intimacy, and the novel *Exclusive.* Her work has been recognized by national magazines, radio, and television.

The Signals Agency, Shiraz's own marketing and management firm, handles corporate clients, events, and media relations.

For more information on Yasmin Shiraz, please visit: www.yasminshiraz.net.